**W9-ABP-282**

# PEOPLE OF THE BOOK

# People of the Book
## Paul Edwards, S.J.

Templegate Publishers

220.46
Ed P

Templegate Publishers
302 E. Adams St./P.O. Box 5152
Springfield, Illinois 62705

ISBN 0-87243-161-4

# Contents

# Introduction

## *Out of the Stained Glass Window*

It was the Year Of Our Lord Nineteen Hundred And Forty, the eighteenth of my own age, and it must have been Ascensiontide, for the Novice's Choir, in which I sang tenor with an unfortunate tendency to tremolo, was preparing for the Feast of Pentecost. The choirmaster handed us some music of a kind unfamiliar to me. 'What is it?', I asked. 'It's a Holy Ghost song.', was the reply. I stared my disapproval, then voiced it. A Holy Ghost song! 'Well, it's about the Holy Ghost.', commented the choirmaster equably. I was not placated. 'Clementine' was a song, and 'There is a Tavern in the Town' and 'The Rose of Tralee.' You could have a hymn to the Holy Ghost, and the word 'motet' sounded suitably solemn and ecclesiastical, but songs were worldly, or, as I would later learn to say, 'profane'. It went without saying that to bring the profane anywhere near the religious, the sacred, was at least irreverent, and, at the worst, blasphemous. So I thought in those far-off, bright-green days, but my choirmaster had, without either of us suspecting it, sown a sturdy, if slow-growing, doubt.

The choirmaster was a man of parts, several years older than myself, a graduate, an experienced teacher, a competent artist and musician. It was some months later that, again unwittingly, he took my education a stage further. Three of us were taking our routine Sunday afternoon walk along the local county lanes, the same roads where Gerard Manley Hopkins had walked and found inspiration for so much of his nature poetry. The choirmaster entertained us with neither sprung rhythm nor talk of inscape, but by retailing to us the story of Esther. He had recently re-read the book, and he told us the story in exactly the same way in which he would have recounted the plot of any other interesting short story. There was no aura of 'Holy Writ' or 'Sacred Scripture'. Esther did not walk through his narrative all soulfulness and sanctity wearing a palpable halo. She was a worried but resourceful young woman, who had been forced to play a game of intrigue for appallingly high stakes against a particularly bloodthirsty but quite credible villain whom, against all the odds, she managed first to outwit and then to destroy.

So I gradually came to see that a hymn is a song quite as much as a love song or drinking chorus, but one which should well up from a deeper level within myself, and that the Bible is, among other things, an anthology of very good stories, to be enjoyed as other stories are, but also to be assimilated into the deeper levels of my mind and heart. It proved harder to apply the second lesson than the first. The initial difficulty was the stiff, antique English mixed with distended Latinisms of the Rheims-Douay version, completed in 1609, the only translation readily available to us. The greater obstacle was the one described by that famous exegete Cecil B. DeMille, as 'that stained-glass telescope which centuries of tradition and form have put between us and the men and women of flesh and blood who lived and wrote the Bible.' A telescope isolates a small circular scene and holds it in unreal detachment from its setting. At the same time it appears to bring the object much nearer to the observer. I should therefore like to amend the great director's phrase, and say that we are in the habit of looking at Bible events through a reversed telescope, which, while holding the events isolated from the rest of reality, also multiplies the distance between the protagonists and ourselves. The epithet 'stained-glass' I like very much. It suggests a general churchiness of atmosphere, the imposition of a predetermined colouring not native to the object, and that air of fixity, of timeless immobility, which the figures in a stained-glass window commonly wear. Prick them, and they could never bleed; tickle them, if you could possibly imagine yourself doing so, and they would prove quite incapable of laughter.

Trying not to tickle, but metaphorically to come to grips with 'the men and women of flesh and blood' in the Bible, to contemplate them without the stained-glass telescope, has become one of the hobbies of my adult life. It is a hobby which has often had to go unindulged over long periods of time, yet never lost anything of its appeal, increased it rather until it has become something of a passion, or in the idiom of our unromantic times, an addiction. It may strike the lay reader as very odd that a priest should describe Scripture study as a hobby, when it is surely one of his primary professional obligations. I am glad that the laity hold that view. When I was a seminarian, Scripture was a Cinderella, shouldered aside by some larger, ugly, but actually much younger sisters, such as Moral Theology, Apologetics and Canon Law. Authority has since declared that Cinderella should not only go to the ball, but that she should return permanently to the palace and receive the full honours of her rank. Unfortunately that rehabilitation came too late for my own particular year, who left the seminary with a detailed knowledge of reserved sins and censures, and three fascicules of notes on the moral obligations arising out of contracts, but without having heard a lecture on the Epistles of St. Paul.

I went from the seminary to be the Senior History Master, and later the Deputy-Head in a Jesuit High School, a situation very little affected either by my fading knowledge of Canon Law, or my lack of instruction in St. Paul. Meanwhile my persistent scrabblings in Scripture during these years began to have a cumulative effect on my preaching, my retreat giving, and, most of all, on my own religious outlook. The significant development came in my fifties, when I was transferred from teaching History to teaching Scripture Knowledge. Ever a conscientious pedagogue, I went to evening classes at the University to revive my Greek. At fifty-five I bought myself a Hebrew grammar and replaced my daily stint of Greek grammar with Hebrew. Yet, although I may now burrow in commentaries, and work laboriously through the Greek or Hebrew text, I have remained obstinately faithful to the light which I began to glimpse on that Sunday afternoon so long ago.

9

A Bible narrative is in the first place a story, one put together, worked over and narrated by practised raconteurs to their contemporaries, who, even when they were literate, were still accustomed to learn far more through their ears than from the written word. I strive to give those story tellers my fullest cooperation. I collect all the background information I can. I ask people who grew up on farms about sheep and crops. I pester equestrians with naive questions about horses in an attempt to understand chariot warfare. I stare at pictures of Egyptian, Assyrian and Canaanite artefacts, when relevant, and study maps of long dead empires. I labour to visualise the scene, to catch its atmosphere, to feel with its characters. If, I believe, I first do all I can to open my imagination to the story, to savour it to the full as a tale, I shall be the more open to digest its teaching into my mind and heart, to assimilate its message into my living. That is the theory behind most of the articles in this book. I try to make the story live for myself in the way I have described, to feel its impact. Then I work like a galley slave, but with typewriter and waste bin, to communicate what I have seen, thought and felt to a literate fellow Christian, largely or wholly innocent of technical Scripture study. I have especially in mind the devout Roman Catholic, sadly conscious of his or her ignorance of the Bible, who has bravely attempted to remedy this lack by starting at Genesis, Chapter I, with the intention of persevering to the end of Revelation, and foundered like an unwatered camel somewhere in the drier reaches of the Pentateuch. I have the temerity to suggest that such a person might do better to read one of these articles, and, if the story catches their imagination, look up the full story in its Bible setting. Then they could repeat the process with some other article which takes their fancy.

The articles were not originally written with any such pedagogical end in view. Early in 1984 the Editor of the British Jesuit publication *The Month* asked me to provide a single page *Reflection* for the first page of the magazine. I wrote about David and Absolom (*Forgiveness*) because the subject interested me. Two months later I was asked to supply another and wrote about Ruth (*Total Commitment*). Then I was asked to supply an article monthly until further notice. At first the subjects were chosen practically at random. I wrote about Judith because the Editor more or less challenged me to; about Rachel to please a lady of that name. Only when it had been suggested that the articles might be collected into a single book did I begin to distribute them more systematically over both Testaments. The order in which they appear here is not the order of their publication. I have arranged them largely in the order in which their subjects can be found in the Catholic Edition of the Revised Standard Version. However, I decided to open with *Forgiveness* followed by *Total Commitment*, they being more characteristic, more generally representative, than those on the Flood or Babel, the latter pair not being centered on a personality, or group of persons, as most of the articles are. We have also included a longer article on Revelation (*Here Be Dragons*) to round off the collection. This originally appeared in *The Way* in October 1981.

I am grateful to the late Hugh Kay, who gave permission for the reprinting of the articles from *The Month*, and to the late Fr. James Walsh, who gave permission for the reprinting of the article from *The Way*. I am grateful to Fr. William Broderick, Director of St. Beuno's Spiritual Exercises Centre, who has allowed me the time to write, and has consistently treated my writing with more respect than I often fear it deserves. I apologise to Catholic readers for a remark in *Elijah's Despair* about Malachi, which ignores the Deuterocanonical Maccabees.

St. Beuno's
CLWYD
September 1986.

# Forgiveness

*'Deal gently with the young man, Absolom.' And all the people heard when the King gave orders to all the commanders about Absolom. (2 Sam. 18.5)*

Was there, I wonder, much sympathy among 'the people' for the King's concern about his son, as they marched out to battle, every man knowing that he might well be dead or maimed before sundown? Nobody on the other side was giving orders to deal gently with *them*! Their only guarantee of staying alive and in one piece was to kill or maim the enemy first. Not Philistines or Amalekites this time, mind you — the King had dealt with them long ago — but fellow Israelites. The King, the smartest commander between the Nile and the Euphrates, and, if anything, rather better at politics, had licked all Israel into one effective kingdom, with the Philistines, Moabites and the rest cowering in their own territories and some even paying to be left alone. Now, thanks to Goldilocks Absolom and his itch to play ruler, it was all coming apart again.

So this morning it was 'kill or be killed', this afternoon too, likely enough. Many a loyal Kingsman would die in the course of the day, and as many of the other side as they could take with them. Even the King, consigned to the comparative safety of the rear, would not survive a victory by Absolom's lot for long. And which was the safest head on both sides? The one with two hundred shekels' weight of hair hanging from it, that of Absolom.

Perhaps similar sentiments were in Joab's mind when, ignoring the King's commands, he sank his three darts into the helpless Absolom and sent in his ten squires to make sure he would never imperil King or Kingdom again.

When nine years before, Absolom had assasinated Amnon, the King's eldest son and ravisher of Absolom's sister, Joab probably admired him for it. This young cub, obviously inheriting from his father more than his good looks, had shown a lot of nerve in striking down the probable heir to the throne, a lot of patience by waiting two years and a very nice grasp of tactics. In the end Amnon had no more chance among Absolom's men than Tamar had had in Amnon's chamber. Then there were three miserable years, with Absolom kicking his heels in Geshur and David yearning his heart out to have him back. It was Joab who had finally persuaded David to let him return to Jerusalem, and Joab again who, at the end of two further years, very frustrating ones for Absolom, had brought him back to court.

For the next four years the unnatural ingrate had stalked the kingship as he had once stalked Amnon. He openly cultivated petitioners on their way to the King, flattering them, kissing them, disparaging his father's administration, while in secret he won over conspirators of real weight, men like the infernally astute Ahitophel. Then, judging himself to have alienated enough of the nation from David, he called a grand celebration at Hebron. At a sheep shearing party nine years ago he had pounced on Amnon; at this celebration he seized the kingship. David had had to fly for his life. He had to leave Jerusalem, and put the Jordan between himself and his parricidal off-spring.

Yet, incredibly, in the eyes of Ahitophel, Absolom had still not gone far enough. Who was to say that David, the incalculable David, who had forgiven the death of his heir, might not forgive a beloved son even rebellion and treachery? Ahitophel said . . . 'Go in to your father's concubines . . . so they pitched a tent for Absolom . . . and Absolom went in to his father's concubines in the sight of all Israel'. This is not so much a gruesome wartime atrocity, it is a ritual act of supplantation and defiance, the deep shame of which David could only dissolve in blood, while Absolom had to destroy his father or else live in lasting fear of his vengeance. The breach between David and his son was now irreparable.

So thought Ahitophel. Wrongly. Even the shrewdest mind in all Israel never conceived that the King might love his son more than his kingship, more than his life, even more than his male honour. When Absolom led in an army to destroy him finally, David said, 'Deal gently with the young man'. When they brought him news from the battlefield his only question was, 'Is it well with the young man Absolom?' When he learned that he and his kingdom were safe and his honour vindicated, but Absolom dead, he abandoned himself to grief, 'Would that I had died instead of you, O Absolom, my son, my son!'

Our favourite illustration of the infinitely loving, forgiving fatherhood of God is the gospel story of the Prodigal Son. I presume to suggest that the story of David and Absolom surpasses it.

For my part, I am fascinated by the fact that Absolom mirrors his father. ('Let us make man in our image, after our likeness'.) He has his father's looks, his daring, his combination of determination and patience, and his ability to charm the public and win over individuals. Then these very gifts are deployed to oust the father ('you will be like God'). The Prodigal Son had squandered a sizeable part of the family property; but there was no question of his supplanting or destroying his father. Measured by the actions of Absolom, his offences look almost venial. The Prodigal presented himself a resourceless and remorseful suppliant. Absolom, possessed of kingship, capital and harem, crossed the Jordan with an army to crush his father.

Absolom's crimes grow in enormity until even David's ablest councillor considers them irredeemable, but David's love proves indestructible, even irreducible, which is why this story is my favourite representation of the endlessly forgiving love of God, and the chief spur to my conscience as to how we should love, how we should forgive, if we are to realise in ourselves the image and likeness of God.

# Total Commitment

*So she went down to the threshing floor and did just as her mother-in-law told her. And when Boaz had eaten and drunk, and his heart was merry, he went to lie at the end of the heap of grain. Then she came softly, and uncovered his feet, and lay down. (Ruth 3.6,7).*

The romantic poet, Victor Hugo, was moved by the lyrical qualities of this scene from the Book of Ruth to write one of his best known works, 'Booz Endormi'. A modern feminist might view the same scene as exhibiting the age-old humiliating predicament of the woman who can only establish her place in society, only be sure of enough to eat, by arousing the sexual interest of a male, first gift-wrapping herself ('Wash therefore and anoint yourself, and put on your best clothes') and approaching her prospect at the moment of least resistance. ('Go down to the threshing floor, but do not make yourself known to the man until he has finished eating and drinking').

More dispassionately, which is not to say more accurately, the anthropologist might note the location (Bethlehem, House of Bread), the actual site (the grain-stacked threshing floor) the season (the end of the grain harvest) and see this encounter of the man of substance and the young woman in terms of a fertility cult.

How, then, is the Christian to read the Hebrew tale of Ruth the Moabitess? First of all, I suggest, we should learn from the anthropologist the vital (quite literally) importance of grain to people for whom meat was an occasional indulgence and the variable milk supply slender at best. The need of grain took Abraham as far as Egypt, as also his great-grandsons, Jacob's brood. It took Elimelech of Bethlehem with his wife,

Naomi, and their two sons eastward into the country of Moab. They lived there long enough for the sons to take local wives, for death to overtake Elimelech, and, more prematurely, both sons, leaving Naomi manless. Here the feminist is correct. Without husband or son Naomi was unprotected, unprovided for, her life, which without children would end with her own, precarious and wholly insignificant. She decides to live out these last years at Bethlehem.

Two resources remain to her, a claim to some land of Elimelech's at Bethlehem, and the deep attachment to her of her daughters-in-law. Unselfishly, Naomi bids them return to their original families, 'The Lord grant that you may find a home, each in the house of her husband'. Both refuse, and it is only when Naomi insists on the hopelessness of a future at Bethlehem that one, Orpah, capitulates. Not so Ruth, the other one. She holds her ground, and when Naomi makes a third plea for her to return to 'her own', Ruth pronounces the most complete statement of irreversible commitment that I know. 'Where you go, I will go, and where you lodge, I will lodge; your people shall be my people, and your God my God; where you die I will die, and there will I be buried.' Do you know any marriage formula, any wording of religious profession, so expressive, so eloquent?

Their lives now inextricably linked, the two childless widows trudge to Bethlehem, where Naomi's contemporaries hesitantly recognise her. 'I went away full', exclaims Naomi to explain the change in herself, 'and the Lord has brought me back empty.' Her remark appears to ignore Ruth, who, to provide sustenance for them both, goes gleaning. This does not mean posing in sweetly paintable rural stances against a flattering background of burnished sheaves. It means incessant stooping under the harvest sun, careful to leave not a single grain-bearing stalk ungathered; starting in the morning and finishing sometime after the reapers have called it a day; then settling down to the monotonous, but at least stationary, labour of beating out the grain.

Boaz, owner of the field and kinsman to Elimelech, notices her, asks who she is and shows himself most considerate. He gives orders that she is not to be molested, that plenty of barley should be left in her path and invites her to share their food, their wine and their water; so Ruth goes back to Naomi with a sizable parcel of barley and even some of her own lunch. The narrator makes it plain that Boaz has been so kindly, not because she has 'taken his fancy', but because 'All that you have done for your mother-in-law since the death of your husband has been fully told me'.

The narrator is careful to stress the same point when Ruth makes her midnight overtures. It is not Naomi's cosmetic ploys which win Boaz, but Ruth's sense of duty. It is her selfless fidelity to the family into which she has married which persuades him to play his own part as kinsman, to take charge of Elimelech's land, to provide for his womenfolk, to prolong the life of the family by fathering the children of one of them.

So there is marriage and a birth. Ruth is transformed from the tolerated immigrant gleaner to the wife of the lord of the harvest and mother of his heir. Naomi, of course, shares in her elevation; indeed, so entwined have their lives now become that the women of Bethlehem say, 'A son has been born to Naomi.' They assure Naomi, 'He shall be to you a restorer of life and a nourisher of your old age.' And they point to the real factor behind her prosperity, 'for your daughter-in-law who loves you, who is more to you than seven sons, has borne him'. Ruth's son, Obed, was an ancestor of David. He was therefore an ancestor of Christ. Naomi was delivered from hunger and childlessness; David delivered Israel from the Philistines, and, at least in his life time, from tribal disunity; Christ offers salvation to the whole of our race. And each form of deliverance can be traced back to the Moabite girl saying 'where you go I will go', back to that gentile woman, widowed and childless, committing her life to another woman, also widowed and childless and a generation older.

In the Book of Ruth I see fertility of field and family as symbols of the profoundly salvific, regenerative power of total self-commitment. In a period when marriage seems so frighteningly fragile, and religious profession so unedifyingly revocable, it might be of special significance.

# Taken at the Flood

*And Noah, he often said to his wife when he sat down to dine, 'I don't care where the water goes if it doesn't get into the wine'.*

Those lines of Chesterton form one of the eight non-biblical quotations in the Oxford Dictionary Of Quotations (1959) on the subject of the Flood. All of them are light-hearted, some downright farcical. This puzzles me. I do not object to the humorous handling of a biblical theme. I believe that if a thing is real, it can stand up to being laughed at; it is only the pretentious and the spurious which have to be protected by a sterile, laughter-free environment of unrelieved solemnity. I am puzzled that the Flood story should generate quite so much levity when it contains some of the grimmest verses in the whole Bible. In fact, when I read it immediately after the description of Creation, I find it almost unbearable.

The Creation story of the Bible's first page always seems to me a happy poetic masque in seven scenes. It is a cosmic spectacular, of which God is simultaneously the author, the producer and the audience, enjoying in all three roles the excellence of His own work. As one would expect in any theatre, the first thing that happens is the illumination of the scene. 'And God said, 'Let there be light'; and there was light. And God saw that the light was good.' However, the scene is not yet set. In this drama it proceeds with stately precision to set itself. A 'firmament' separates the 'waters which were under the firmament from the waters which were above the firmament', and then 'the waters under the firmament' gather together and the dry land appears.

This 'dry land' is the platform upon which Man will act his part, but first the earth must be enriched with plants and fruit trees, the sea with 'swarms of living creatures', the sky be criss-crossed by birds, and the sun, the moon and the stars set in the firmament to irradiate the whole. The animals take their places, and then God says, 'Let us make man in our image, after our likeness.' So God created man in his own image, in the image of God he created him'. Six times in the course of the action we hear the lyrical refrain: 'And God saw that it was good'. Finally: 'And God saw everything that he had made, and behold, it was very good.' So the seventh 'day' God devotes to tranquil, satisfied repose.

Having savoured the joyousness of that story I need turn only a single page in my edition of the Bible, to read in Chapter 6: 'Now the earth was corrupt in God's sight, and the earth was filled with violence.' Three such statements have taken the place of 'God saw that it was good'. The source of this corruption is the human race. 'The earth is filled with violence through them.' 'The wickedness of man was great upon the earth . . . every imagination of the thoughts of his heart was only evil continually.' So much for 'the image and likeness' of God! The Creator's pleasure in His own handi-work has turned to bitter regret. 'And the Lord was sorry that he had made man upon the earth, and it grieved him to his heart. "I am sorry that I have made them."'" In utter revulsion He declares, 'I will blot out man whom I have created . . . I will destroy them with the earth . . . Every living thing that I have made I will blot out from the face of the ground.'

The execution of this desolate decree repeats to quite an extent the stages of creation, systematically reversing its achievements. Thus: 'on that day all the fountains of the great deep burst forth and the windows of heaven were opened' i.e. the waters which were separated on the second day into those 'under the firmament' and those 'above the firmament' have now been released from their bounds and anarchically mingle once again. 'The waters under the heaven' thus reinforced and no longer 'gathered into one place' overwhelm the dry land. 'And the waters prevailed so mightily upon the earth that all the high mountains under the whole heaven were covered.' Life is extinguished. 'And all flesh died that moved upon the earth, birds, cattle, beasts, all swarming creatures . . . and every man.' Twice in the relevant passage in Chapter 7 we are told that all living things died; twice that they were 'blotted out'.

Contemplating this universal destruction my mind goes back to the charge: 'the earth is filled with violence through them.' 'Violence' covers much more than physical assault. The Hebrew word includes false accusations, the perversion of justice, the callous exploitation of the weak, especially of the widow and orphan, the usurpation and unscrupulous infringement of the rights of others, both of God and of man. Where 'violence' is rife we kill and starve one another; we extinguish animal species, disrupt the ecology, pollute the atmosphere and the rivers, and are equipped and poised to destroy a hemisphere in a matter of hours.

I admit that in these paragraphs on the Flood I have ignored the covenant with Noah and neglected the new beginning which a merciful Creator thus provided for the world, first cleansing it of the corruption with which man had filled it. These are important, even indispensable, considerations. Yet I suggest that we should not pass on to them until we have brooded long upon our ability to deface in ourselves the divine image and to wreck our own habitat. I recall that when Jonah, who like Noah was preserved in 'the heart of the seas', warned Nineveh of its imminent destruction, the King of Nineveh decreed: 'let everyone turn from his evil way and from the violence which is in his hands. Who knows, God may yet repent and turn from his fierce anger so that we perish not.'

# Tower of Babel

*Then they said, 'Come, let us build ourselves a city, and a tower with its top in the heavens, and let us make a name for ourselves, lest we be scattered abroad on the face of the earth.' (Gen. 11.4.)*

If you attend mass on Pentecost Eve, or on the Friday of the Sixth Week of the Year (Year 1), you will hear the story of the Tower of Babel. A children's fable, you may think or, more precisely, a tale conceived when men's minds and imaginations functioned at a very childlike level. Start to read the comments of the biblical scholars, and you have to revise your opinion as you begin to appreciate the narrative techniques and paronomastic skill employed. For instance, the very name of the abandoned city, BaBeL, puns with the Hebrew verb BaLaL, to confuse, while 'BaBel' is also the Hebrew version of the name 'Babylon', so that the story cocks a very deliberate snook at that ancient seat of Empire, a gesture all the more appreciated by a Jewish audience during and after the Babylonian captivity. In the development of the tale there is a very subtle structure of parallels, contrasts and reversals. In the Hebrew wording there are puns, assonances and quite elaborate patterns of sound. The central imagery may be ingenuous (and consequently memorable?), but the fabulist's literary powers are considerable.

It is entirely appropriate that they should be, because the story he is telling is, I would make bold to claim, one of the most important in the whole Bible. To gauge this, look at the situation at the beginning, and then at the end. At the start, the people enjoy unity in every respect. They are all in one place; they all speak one language; they concur and cooperate in a single project. At the end, they have 'left off building the city'; they do not 'understand one another's speech'; and the Lord has 'scattered them abroad over the face of all the earth'. This is a 'Fall' story, only a little less significant than the Garden of Eden myth. In 'the garden' man lived harmoniously with God, with his wife and with nature. His sin damages all three relationships. God kindly runs him up some fur or leather gear, but can no longer tolerate him in 'the garden'. The woman, the man blames, and will dominate. Nature grown grudging, may yield him sustenance for his brief life, but will make him sweat for it. In the Babel story a similar 'fall' takes place in human society, and also in three respects. The people cease to live together, to work together, to understand one another.

There is the same cause behind the degeneration of the man's relationships in Eden, and the disintegration of the polity of Babel. In 'the garden' the forbidden fruit is 'good for food' and 'a delight to the eye', but the inducement, which the serpent in his cunning holds out, is 'your eyes will be opened, and you will be like God'. At Babel, the group fears for its own dissolution, 'lest we be scattered abroad', and their insurance against such fate is 'to make a name for ourselves'. This they will achieve by building 'a city and a tower with its top in the heavens'. 'The heavens', of course, are the realm of the deity — 'No man has ascended into heaven, but he who descended from heaven, the Son of Man.' Both Adam and the Babel-onians ignore God. Adam and Eve disregard His prohibition; the folk of Babel try to assert and preserve their corporate identity without any reference to Him. The former aspired to be like God; the latter prepare to trespass on His domain. Of Adam, God says, 'the man has become like one of us'; of the 'Babel-onians, 'nothing that they propose to do will now be impossible for them'. He speaks with a disdainful, Olympian irony. Both sets of human beings have ignored God, have grossly overreached themselves, have arrogantly, though impotently, challenged the cosmic order.

In the Genesis stories God punishes their hubristic presumption. In fact, arrogance, folly and self-worship rebound on the perpetrator without the need of direct divine intervention. What I find of special interest in the Babel story is the form which God's alleged intervention takes. 'The Lord confused the language of all the earth'. If they are unable to communicate, it no longer matters whether people live cheek by jowl or inhabit separate continents. Each individual has become a remote inaccessible island and cooperation is ruled out. Once their language is 'confused', the Babel-onian community is already dissolved and their grandiose project cancelled.

'The fall' leads, in God's mercy, to the Redemption, and at this stage of the scriptural narrative, Babel acquires a new relevance. We read in the Acts of the Apostles that when the gospel was first preached, it was to a cosmopolitan crowd, with people from as far afield as Persia, Mesopotamia, Libya and Rome, and 'each one heard them speaking in his own tongue'. That was only the beginning of the reversal of Babel. Those who believed 'devoted themselves to the apostles' teaching and fellowship'. That 'fellowship', one might say 'community', is further described; 'And all who believed were together, and had all things in common . . . attending the temple together and breaking bread in their homes.' The Redemption, at work among the believers, is described, not in terms of the reversal of the expulsion from Eden, but as a rectification of Babel.

The first believers created a community at least as united as that of Babel before the Fall, but with at least two important differences. First, they are not intent on making a name for themselves. They had been 'baptized every one in the name of Christ'; they held that 'there is no other name given among men by which we might be saved'. Secondly, they do not see themselves as pioneers achieving 'the heavens'. Christ had 'descended from heaven' and was now 'exalted at the right hand of God'. He was the tower between heaven and earth. He is the 'True Babel,' for — I have kept this fact in reserve — in its Assyrian form the term meant 'Gate of God'. We Christians are the New Babel-onians, called to build a city in the form of human community, as wide as the world itself, around a Tower already in position. Remembering the first Babel, let us mind our language, its vitality, its expressiveness, its effectiveness.

# Jacob's Web

*Jacob said to his father, 'I am Esau your first born. I have done as you told me; now sit up and eat of my game, that you may bless me' (Genesis 27.19).*

Jacob, of course, is lying his young head off. In fact, he stands there in front of his blind father like some sort of monument in duplicity, posing as Esau in Esau's best clothes, his neck and wrists wrapped in kidskin which the kids themselves were wearing earlier in the day. Even the dish he is offering is part of the fraud. It is a goat-meat which his mother Rebecca has disguised to taste like one of Esau's game stews, just as she has dressed up Jacob as his elder brother.

Jacob moves through the consequent interview as through a minefield, temporarily disarming each mine with another lie. 'How is it you have found it so quickly?' asks Isaac. Jacob may have been ready for that one. He had to come suspiciously early rather than risk Esau turning up in the middle of the scene. 'Because the Lord your God granted me success'. Was Esau always so piously modest about his hunting triumphs? Perhaps not, as Isaac is plainly suspicious. 'Come near that I may feel you'. How Jacob must have hoped that the kidskins would do the trick, and that they would stay in place. They did. Isaac is still not wholly convinced. 'The voice is Jacob's voice, but the hands are the hands of Esau'. Jacob was probably having enough trouble making his voice sound normal, without trying to do an imitation of Esau's. Isaac tries a direct appeal, 'Are you really my son Esau?' Did Jacob try to sound like Esau this time when he said, 'I am'?

Defeated, if not convinced, the old man takes the food, no doubt masticating it with all the deliberation of the aged, while

Jacob stands by hoping that his mother's mock venison ragout will, like himself, escape detection. At last, the undetected goatflesh washed down by genuine wine, Isaac is ready to confer the blessing. 'Come near and kiss me, my son'. One hopes that this was Jacob's worst moment. The solemn blessing is ritually given, invoking both prosperity: 'plenty of grain and wine', and hegemony: 'may your mother's sons bow down to you'. Then Jacob can hurry off to get out of Esau's clothes before Esau finds him in them. The blessing, in Hebrew thought, remains with him, as presumably does the guilt.

As to his guilt, how grave should we judge it? Before the twins were born, Rebekah had consulted an oracle and been told, 'the elder shall serve the younger'. For her, then, as for Jacob, the senior's blessing was his by divine decree. Esau had preceded him into the world by a matter of minutes at most. Were those minutes to relegate him to life-long inferiority, and his sons after him? Rebekah much preferred Jacob, and wanted him to have the precedence the oracle had promised, but her woman's views carried no weight, although she had carried the weight of the twins themselves throughout an agonising pregnancy. Isaac, unchallengeable patriarch, would follow tradition, especially as he loved the extrovert, self-indulgent, somewhat obtuse Esau. When a man is consigned by a ruling convention to a position of irrevocable inferiority, when a woman is rendered powerless by a patriarchal system in a matter of importance to her, what can they do? They can observe the weaknesses of those in control, and then muster their own ingenuity, skill and nerve to exploit the opportunities thus offered. Rebekah had done just that, and very effectively, although, like many another strong-minded woman, she had had to leave the execution of her stratagem to a less resolute male.

It is little benefit she has of it in the Genesis story. She despatches Jacob to her brother, hundreds of miles to the North, out of reach of Esau's vengeance, never, apparently, to see him again. She remains with the aged husband she has tricked, and the son she has robbed and the Hittite daughters-in-law she detested. Jacob trudges to the Euphrates, solitary and resourceless, to begin a twenty-year exile as a hireling shepherd with his Uncle Laban, his hire for the first seven years being the prospect of marriage with his cousin, Rachel, to whom he has lost his heart. At the end of the seven years the wedding celebrations take place. That night, as Rebekah had once sent Jacob instead of Esau to be blessed by his sightless father, so Laban, her brother, leads, not Rachel, but her elder sister Leah to the nuptial tent, to the expectant Jacob, unseeing in its dark interior.

Next morning Laban justifies himself to the indignant Jacob. 'It is not so done in our country to give the younger before the elder'. The principle that Rebekah and Jacob deceived Isaac to circumvent, Laban had deceived Jacob to implement — as neat a piece of poetic justice as you could wish. A postscript to the story is Jacob's meeting with Esau after twenty years. Esau proves entirely welcoming, generous and solicitous. Jacob, very apprehensive, very wary, approaches him 'bowing himself to the ground seven times'. So much for the blessing, 'may your mother's sons bow down to you'. He declines Esau's protection and separates from him as soon as politeness permits. It is the deceiver, not the unvindictive victim, who is incapable of trust. 'Oh what a tangled web we weave . . .'

Isaac, Rebekah, Esau and Jacob, are really quite good people, I think. Yet Isaac and Esau unthinkingly follow a system which Rebekah and Jacob have good reason to resent. When Rebekah and Jacob unite to cheat the system, they seem to inflict more harm upon themselves than on the cheated. Nobody in the situation is wholly blameless, nobody entirely guilty. In the Gospels, by contrast, there seem to be three classes of people: the good, the bad but repentant, the obstinately bad. I find the Old Testament more realistic. As a rough rule of thumb take your ideals from the New Testament and your picture of human nature from the Old. The combination may save us . . . as it was meant to do.

# Romance of Rachel

*Now when Jacob saw Rachel the daughter of Laban his mother's brother, and the sheep of Laban . . . Jacob went up and rolled the stone from the well's mouth, and watered the flock of Laban . . . Then Jacob kissed Rachel and wept aloud. And Jacob told Rachel that he was Rebekah's son; and she ran and told her father (Genesis 29:10-2).*

As Laban listened to his excited daughter he must have felt that he was hearing this story for the second time. So had his sister Rebekah come running home from the well to tell them of the master of a well-found camel train, who had courteously asked her for a drink. When the obliging girl had poured water not only for him, but for the whole string of ten camels, he had rewarded her with a fine gold ring and two handsome gold bracelets. Coming to the house he had announced himself to be the servant of their kinsman Abraham and asked for Rebekah as a bride for Abraham's son and heir. When the family agreed, he had borne her away south the very next day, leaving them all with some costly ornaments and a family legend of the whirlwind wooing of Rebekah.

Now Laban's own daughter has come home starry-eyed and babbling about another impressive stranger at the well who was claiming membership of the family. It was not exactly Rebekah's story over again. This man was not a superior servant, but a young man of lineage. Abraham's grandson, his own nephew apparently. On the other hand, there was no camel train and no sign of gold ornaments. The lone traveller had not asked Rachel for water, but had wrenched aside the massive stone cover unaided, and gone on to perform himself the laborious chore of drawing up water for the whole of

33

Rachel's flock. This he had followed up by kissing her and bursting into tears. Naturally, young Rachel had found this display of youthful strength, gallantry, ardour and sensibility more fascinating than any gold ring or pair of bracelets. Was this man also seeking a bride?

He was. Rebekah had sent him north, partly to escape Esau's vengeance, partly to find a wife of their own stock. Having met Rachel, Jacob's heart was wholly set on marrying her. This time, however there was no impromptu betrothal, no claiming of the betrothed the next day. It was agreed between them that Jacob should work for Laban for seven years and then marry Rachel. The seven years 'seemed to him but a few days because of the love he had for her'. Did the time pass equally swiftly for Rachel? We are not told. Nor do we know how long before the marriage she learned that it was not herself, but her unattractive elder sister Leah, whom Laban intended to place in Jacob's marriage tent. Did she know that Laban proposed to offer her as a second wife in return for another seven year's service? Was she confident that Jacob's love was powerful enough for him to swallow his anger and his humiliation and meet Laban's terms? The Hebrew author pays her no attention at this stage, focussing solely on the duel between Laban and Jacob. Jacob, far from home, inexperienced, empty-handed and in love is easy meat for Laban, the old hand, on his own ground, disposing of flocks and marriageable daughters. Jacob has bid very high for Rachel and has been tricked into accepting Leah as well, at the same high price.

The two women share Jacob in a way bitterly unsatisfactory to both. Rachel has his love; Leah bears his children. Leah, who plainly has the author's sympathy, gives birth to a series of lusty sons, always hoping that they will establish her in Jacob's heart. Rachel, desperately unhappy, has recourse to her people's form of surrogate motherhood; 'Here is my maid Bilhah; go into her . . . that I may have children through her'. Jacob consents, and has two sons by Bilhah, to Rachel's satisfaction, 'I have wrestled with my sister and have prevailed'. Leah in response employs the same tactic, and her maid Zilpah similarly bears two boys, while Leah herself subsequently has two more sons, thus firmly consolidating her advantage. Then Rachel at last conceives, and blissfully gives birth in the cheerful hope that this will not be her only child, 'May the Lord add to me another son'.

If the two women are locked in an ongoing struggle with one another, they are as one when it comes to standing behind Jacob in the second part of his contest with their father. I find the story very obscure. The contractual arrangements are vague; the ovine and caprine genetics involved not really credible. Jacob is plainly thriving, but it is in spite of Laban's chicanery, and Jacob yearns for independence. The sisters give him every encouragement. 'Are we not regarded by him as foreigners? For he has sold us, and he has been using up the money'. Jacob departs, and Rachel makes a special contribution to their joint prosperity by carrying off Laban's household gods, which would have been small, precious and prestigious objects. The rigid, aniconic monotheism of Judaism still lay in the future.

Jacob breaks free of his father-in-law only to face his elder brother from whom he had fled twenty years before. His tactics at this hair-raising confrontation declare his priorities. Bilhah and Zilpah are with their offspring in the forward companies, Leah and her six sons come behind, and Rachel, the beloved, with her precious infant, are in comparative safety at the rear. To Jacob's relief, Esau proves not only forgiving, but even welcoming, and so Jacob can enjoy his new independence and growing prosperity unthreatened. In this auspicious setting Rachel conceives again. Her dearest hope is fulfilled in the birth of Benjamin, but the birthpangs had been severe, and Rachel, the ever-cherished wife, now the mother of sons, breathes her last.

An impetuous courtship and a long delayed marriage; the reassurance of love with the frustration of childlessness; her envy of the sister who had good reason to be jealous of her; the fulfilment of her hopes coinciding with her own dissolution. Rachel's story is fascinating in its counterpoint, all woven round the theme of Jacob's love, constant from the afternoon when he lifted the well cover till the day when he raised her memorial cairn. Where the father of the Chosen People gave his heart, we must surely pay the tribute of our respect. Is it part of the point and counterpoint that it was Leah the Unloved who is the ancestress of Moses, of David and of Christ?

# One Tests Ten:
# Survival for Twelve

*Then they took Joseph's robe, and killed a goat, and dipped the robe in the blood . . . and brought it to their father and said, 'This we have found; see now whether it is your son's robe or not'. And he recognised it and said, 'It is my son's robe; a wild beast has devoured him; Joseph is without doubt torn to pieces'. (Genesis 37.31-4)*

Jacob had once stood in front of his own father, wearing his elder brother's best clothes, with goatskin round his neck and wrists, and succeeded in passing himself off as Esau, the elder. Now it is a younger brother's best garment, generously daubed with goat's blood, which lends verisimilitude to a doubtful narrative, as Jacob himself is lied to by ten sons at once. It is not mere numbers which make the second scene the more intense. Isaac's preparance for Esau, his first born, the extrovert out-of-doors man, who provided tasty game dishes, sounds quite venial. In contrast, Jacob's absorption in young Joseph was consistent, conspicuous and to his elder brothers outrageous. Leah's six sons knew that their mother was an elder daughter, that she was the senior wife by seven years and that Jacob's heart was monopolised by her younger sister, Rachel. Their very names (Genesis 29.31 ff.) reflected Leah's pathetic hope, reviving at each birth, that her motherhood of sons might win her some place in her husband's affections. Now they had to watch Rachel's brat swanning around in a tunic fit for a nobleman. The four sons of the bondswomen had their own grievance. Joseph had been carrying tales about them to their father.

Having managed to unite all ten half-brothers against him,

Joseph exasperates them further by cockily rehearsing his dreams. In his first dream they were harvesting together, 'and lo, my sheaf arose and stood upright; and behold, your sheaves . . . bowed down to my sheaf'. In the second dream: 'behold, the sun, the moon and eleven stars were bowing down to me'. Even the doting Jacob was annoyed this time. These people took dreams very seriously, and there was but one obvious way to block their fulfilment. 'Come now, let us kill him . . . and we shall see what will become of his dreams'. Two of the seniors recoil from the bloodshedding. Reuben, the eldest, urges them to leave him marooned in a dry cistern, secretly hoping to extricate him later. Judah persuades them to sell him to a passing caravan en route for Egypt. So Joseph passes out of their lives, they think for ever, while his half-brothers fabricate the evidence of his demise by bloodying his up-market tunic.

Joseph is wearing an even more elegant garment 'of fine linen', and perhaps his gold chain of office, when the Ten enter his presence more than twenty years later, and bow down before him 'with their faces to the ground'. They are quite unaware that this Vizier of All Egypt is the brother they sold into slavery, and that his first dream is being fulfilled by their obeisance. Nor is it easy for us to see the spoiled, loose-tongued youth of two decades before, in this self-possessed man of affairs. Joseph has been schooled in exile and ser-vitude, in approval and responsibility followed by false accusation and imprisonment, and then abruptly elevated to the highest responsibility.

When Jacob's daughter, Dinah, had been ravished by a Cananite, some of her brothers, had resorted to butchery and pillage to avenge her. In contrast, their uncle Esau, whom Jacob had impersonated and cheated of his first-born's bless-ing, when he later encountered Jacob and his family, did not, as Jacob feared, 'slay us all', but 'ran to meet him, fell on his neck and kissed him'. Now that he has all ten brothers in his power, which family precedent will Joseph follow, that of wholesale revenge or signal magnanimity? Both courses are too impulsive, too unconsidered for the judicious administrator which Joseph has become. His conduct is deliberate and exploratory, revealing nothing, in no way committing himself. He charges them with being spies, and so needles them into loquacity about their background; they are 'the sons of one man', one brother being dead, and the youngest with their father in Canaan. Joseph seizes on the last point. Let them produce the youngest brother and they will be believed. He will hold Simeon in prison until they do. Joseph's deliberation is not effortless. At one point he has to break off the audience to weep, and the brothers are sent off with full grain bags and the purchase money surreptitiously returned. Joseph remains au fond a visceral Hebrew.

The plan to bring Benjamin to Egypt hangs fire. With Joseph gone, and now Simeon, Jacob obstinately refuses to risk Benjamin, until the tightening noose of the persistent famine constrains him to yield. Arriving again in Egypt, the brothers are bidden to a banquet with Joseph, who, at the sight of his full brother, is again forced to leave the chamber to seek relief in tears. Nor can he resist sending Benjamin portions from his own table five times the size of those his elders receive. Yet he proceeds with his scheme. His silver divining cup is smuggled into Benjamin's grain bag and in due course discovered there by Joseph's steward. Distraught, the brothers throw themselves at Joseph's feet and invite a corporate punishment. 'We are my lord's slaves, both we and he also in whose hands the cup has been found.' Joseph declines. 'Only the man in whose hand the cup was found shall be my slave; but as for you, go up in peace to your father'.

Joseph has reproduced the situation of twenty years before. Then these half-brothers had callously consigned him to slavery. Now they are offered their own freedom at the price of abandoning Rachel's other child, Jacob's other idolised son, to exactly the same fate. They refuse. Judah who had said of Joseph, 'Come, let us sell him to the Ishmaelites', now pleads urgently and movingly for Benjamin; 'his brother is dead, and he alone is left of his mother's children; and his father loves him', and for Jacob; 'as his life is bound up with the lad's life . . . he will die'. His conclusion 'Let your servant remain instead of the lad as a slave to my lord; and let the lad go back with his brothers'.

These progenitors of the Chosen People are men of deep, and potentially lethal passion. Jacob's flagrant favoritism induces bitter hostility towards the lad he would most cherish. The Ten, or most of them, are violent and ruthless in the vindication of their pride. Joseph's youthful hubris puts him in mortal danger. Thanks to Reuben's humanity he survives to undergo a profound mental metamorphosis. At the same time the Ten, under what benign influence I cannot say, develop a capacity for compassion and even altruism. Without these changes the Children of Israel would have had no future. Is not this the situation of the Family of Man?

# Moses I:
# Light on Two Identities

*Lo, the bush was burning, yet it was not consumed. And Moses said, 'I will turn aside and see this great sight, why this bush is not burned' (Exod. 3.2, 3)*

Walking, I like to imagine, with the unhurried but purposeful gait, which he had learned from the Midianite nomads, Moses made his way across the bone-hard terrain to investigate this mysterious fire, cheerfully unaware that he was about to encounter the far more awesome mystery of the God of Israel. What notion did Moses have, I wonder, of that God? As the adopted son of an Egyptian princess he had presumably learned something of the complex cosmoganies of Memphis and Thebes, and shared in the worship of Ptah, or Horus, or Amon-Re and of those strange, theriomorphic deities of Egypt's multiple theologies. Surrendered to an Egyptian household as soon as weaned, he could have absorbed nothing of his own people's patriarchal pieties. On the other hand, it is hard to credit that as an adult he had become so involved with the Hebrews as to kill in their defence, and yet had learned nothing of their religious traditions. Now an exile among the Midianites, and son-in-law to their priest, he must have taken part in the clan rituals of this, the third people to which he had belonged.

Belonged! Did he belong anywhere? Life as an Egyptian princeling had come to an end when he had 'wasted' that Egyptian bully. At the time he had thought by concealing the corpse to preserve his Egyptian status while being accepted among the Hebrews as a hero and protector. The illusion had lasted a day. This time the bully was himself a Hebrew. Rebuked by Moses for wronging a brother Hebrew, the man had counter-attacked: 'Who made you a prince and judge over us? Do you mean to kill me as you killed the Egyptian?' His cover jeopardised by the very people he had killed for, Moses had fled east. Perhaps he was lucky to be still alive. He did not feel very lucky, trailing across this god-forsaken wilderness with a pack of stupid animals, each of which had the benefit of four legs to his weary two, and not a beast among them his own! He was a man without land or livestock, without place or people, and with no purpose except to survive. He was as astray in life as some of those grass-guzzling quadrupeds would be if left alone for long.

Moses himself was never to be left alone again during the rest of his life. 'Moses, Moses!', came the call from within the blazing, but unscorched, thicket. This is the compelling, iterated summons which was to be heard long after by Samuel, priest, prophet and kingmaker of Israel, and by Saul of Tarsus, Apostle to All the World. The voice proclaims its identity: 'I am the God of your father, the God of Abraham . . .'; expresses a profound, compassionate involvement with Israel: 'I have seen the affliction of *my* people'; and announces the imminent transformation of their lot: 'I am come to deliver them out of the hand of the Egyptians, and to bring them . . . to a good and broad land flowing with milk and honey'. Moses stands at a respectful distance, his feet now reverentially unshod, his burnous pulled across his face 'for he was afraid to look at God'. He now knows with unnerving clarity what Deity controls events, and what shape He intends to give them, and is about to learn his own role therein. 'Come, I will send you to Pharaoh that you may bring forth my people, the sons of Israel, out of Egypt'.

In the Hebrew Moses' immediate protest rings like an agonised squeal, 'Who am I that I should go to Pharoah?' Yet it states only half his fears. Not only must he appear in Pharaoh's eyes a renegade and a murderer, but to his fellow

Hebrews, he is an Egyptianised upstart whose patronage they have already rejected. Is he then to present himself to Pharaoh as a divine emissary, to the Hebrews as a Godsent deliverer? The God does not dispute the double disqualification. Its irrelevance to Omnipotence is simply assumed in the reply, 'But I will be with you'. Moses now switches to the second part of his problem, the Hebrews. 'If they ask me, "What is his name", what shall I say?' The answer is threefold. "I AM WHO I AM...Say...I AM has sent me to you...Say...JHWH, the God of your Fathers, has sent me to you".' Exegetes and theologians commenting on these verses have spilled enough ink to float a tanker, and no doubt, the word processors of their successors will spew forth a large enough mass of printouts to sink it again. Suffice it to observe here that the triple answer insists on the profound actuality of God ('I am really there') and associates with that reality both His relationship with Israel and the mission He has given to Moses.

Moses, still apparently more dismayed by that mission than overawed by the sender, persists with his objections. 'But behold, they will not believe me'. He is then given three impressive powers: to turn a staff into a serpent and back, to make leprosy appear and disappear, to turn Nile water into blood. Wielding visual aids of that calibre a man should be able to sway any audience, yet Moses still pleads that he is underequipped. 'Oh, my Lord, I am not eloquent . . . I am slow of speech and of tongue'. The reply: 'Who has made man's mouth? I will be with your mouth and teach you what you shall speak'. Moses has now advanced four objections, four promising escape routes, only to have each of them countered by massive reassurance, each route blocked by something on the scale of the Great Pyramid. Naked of further pretext, he emits a last quivering appeal, 'Oh, my Lord, send, I pray, some other person'.

He still has to go. He goes from being a man without a people to become the effective founder of the most significant nation in history, from participating in other people's cults to be the mediator of JHWH's covenant with Israel. Even in the Book of the New Covenant no other name, except that of Jesus, will occur as often as that of Moses.

# Moses II:
# Pity My Leader

*Moses heard the people weeping throughout their families, every man at the door of his tent. (Num 11.10)*

A very dispiriting sound for the leader of a people to have to listen to! Every man weeping at the door of his tent, the women within outwailing their menfolk, while the children enter into the spirit of the occasion and sob their little hearts out! And why? Were the chariots of Pharaoh circling round the camp awaiting the signal to race in and slaughter every last Hebrew? Had someone reported the approach of a horde of Amalekites on its way to pillage and slay? Or was there a plague abroad among the tents, with its victims dying off like flies? Nothing quite so hair-raising. The Israelites wanted some adjustments to their diet. 'O that we had meat to eat! We remember the fish we ate in Egypt for nothing, the cucumbers, the melons, the leeks, the onions and the garlic; but now . . . there is nothing but this manna'. There had been similar complaints further back along the route. 'In the land of Egypt . . . we sat by the fleshpots and ate bread to the full'. The forced labour battalions of the Nile Delta, to judge by these nostalgic evocations, must have had remarkably lavish catering arrangements. In fact, one wonders what attraction such pampered palates could find in the thought of a land flowing merely with milk and honey.

Sheer monotony of menu was not, I imagine, the root of this general demoralisation. It sprang, I suggest, from a much deeper malaise, born of their uprooting, their continual, if erratic, movement, the uncertainty of the water supply, the food supply and the route, their misgivings as to whether they were really getting any nearer to Canaan and as to whether, if they reached it at all, they would prove capable to wresting such a land from its present occupants. The tedium of their daily fare has only provided a focus for their general misery. More simply, it was 'the last straw'. Unfortunately it was also the last straw for their leader. Moses, as in every cisis, has recourse to the Lord. Usually he goes to beg for aid or counsel, often to avert His wrath from delinquent Israel. This time he is there to submit his resignation. 'Thou dost lay the burden of all this people upon me . . . Did I conceive all this people? Did I bring forth that thou shouldst say to me, "Carry them in your bosom, as the nurse carries the suckling child?" . . . The burden is too heavy . . . kill me at once, that I may not see my wretchedness'. The Israelites have had a surfeit of manna. Moses has had more than his fill of Israel.

How galling for him to reflect that he could have severed himself from his people for ever, immediately he was weaned! As the adopted son of an Egyptian princess he could be living the elegant, stimulating life of a high-ranking Egyptian, instead of sharing the cloddish existence of these displaced herdsmen. The Egyptians were masters of a large part of the earth; they conceived and executed vast projects; they commissioned all manner of artefacts from gigantic statuary to delicate jewellery, employed painters and musicians. They had their deeds commemorated in finely chiselled masonry and their thoughts recorded on papyrus by deft-fingered secretaries. They had created an extensive and varied literature. The lore of the Hebrews seemed restricted to the pasturing and breeding of cattle, goats and sheep, with a sideline in brickmaking under Egyptian supervision. And they could tell you long, unedifying stories about their ancestors, especially that consummate trickster, Jacob, who had callously deceived his old father, cheated his brother and yet been led up the garden path by his father-in-law to quite the wrong girl. Moses preferred stories about Jacob's son, Joseph, who had risen to be Vizier of All Egypt and had nobly forgiven the half-brothers who had sold him into slavery. His one mistake had been to settle the whole clan in Egypt, so that he, Moses, had had to lead the whole swollen brood of their descendants out again.

Moses had wrecked his own chances of being Vizier, or anything like it, when in loyalty to his Hebrew blood he had killed that brute of an Egyptian. His reward, the first of many sour experiences with his people, had been to have one of them throw the killing in his face, along with the challenge, 'Who made you a prince and judge over us?' To that question Moses now has a divinely dictated answer, 'I AM has sent me'. I AM had sent him, in spite of argument and entreaty, to face Pharaoh and to shepherd the Sons of Israel from Goshen to Canaan, or rather, in his own words, to 'carry them as a nurse carries the suckling child'. But an unweaned child does not turn on you with bitter denunciation at the sight of the Egyptian army, nor accuse you of bringing it into the wilderness to kill it with hunger, nor come near to stoning you because it is thirsty. Still less is it likely, while you are listening to God declare 'You shall have no other gods before me', to be busy moulding a graven image, sacrificing to it and holding an orgy in its honour. Nor does a nurse expect the terrifying experience of having to stand between her charge and the blazing, lethal anger of God.

Moses will go on. The Israelites will reach Canaan, enter it, and settle in it, there to be a free, landed people. A happy ending after all? No, merely the next chapter of a story which continues to unfold. Moses could never have forseen that the literature of Egypt would be of interest to us largely for the light it casts on the literature of Israel, an indispensable part of our Bible, the most translated book in the world. The high civilisation of Egypt, from which Moses was 'untimely ripped', is long dead, but the story of the Chosen People has come to involve us all. When you respond to the call of God you may become as despondent as the Israelites, as heartsick as Moses. What you achieve may be of a quality you cannot conceive, and have effect in dimensions of which you have not dreamed. So, go on. And 'en route' think kindly of those who are called upon to lead.

# Moses III:
# Michelangelo's Mistake

*And Moses went up from the plains of Moab to Mount Nebo, to the top of Pisgah... and the Lord showed him all the land... And the Lord said to him, 'This is the land of which I swore to Abraham, to Isaac and to Jacob, "I will give it to your descendants". I have let you see it with your eyes, but you shall not go over there'. So Moses the servant of the Lord died there in the land of Moab (Deut 34-1.5).*

It was a richly diverse territory which Moses' eyes, old, but quite undimmed, beheld from Pisgah. In the distance lay the Mediterranean; in the foreground the deep sunken valley where the waters of the Jordan ran down to a lifeless sea. Between were the coastal plain, gently sloping hillsides, high plateaux, stark mountain-sides and precipitous escarpments. It seemed more than a lifetime since the Voice from the Burning Bush had declared, 'I have seen the affliction of my people . . . and I have come to deliver them . . . and to bring them . . . to a good and broad land, a land flowing with milk and honey'. There in front of him was that land, and beneath him on the plains of Moab were gathered the freed Sons of Israel, poised to enter therein, not as invaders, but as the rightful heirs, come to claim, to occupy, to enjoy their own.

What sights those aged eyes had looked upon since he had veiled them in awe beside that flaming thicket in Midian! Impelled by the God, who had listened to all his excuses and accepted none, he had been forced to see again the stately halls of Egyptian overlords, where he was reckoned a renegade, a murderer and an agitator. He had had to meet the mistrustful gaze of his fellow Hebrews as he summoned them to follow him to far Canaan and to make it their own. He had watched the chivalry of Egypt drown, every man and horse drown, without a blow struck, and then looked on as the Hebrew women rattled their tambourines exultantly, and danced and chanted in celebration. He had stood clutching the tablets, fresh-incised by Yahweh Himself, and seen the same people perform much the same antics around their molten calf. He had had to stare them down when they were sullen and demoralised, panic-sticken or mutinous. Worst of all were the occasions when he had faced on their behalf the incandescent anger of outraged Godhead.

How indignant this people had been when the Egyptians had demanded that they make bricks without straw! His own Taskmaster had presented him with these descendants of wayward nomads, these exploited helots, and required him to make of them an effective and independent nation, a commonwealth whose moral calibre should not be unworthy of the Lord who called them 'my people'. He had duly led them out of Egypt, shepherded them through hundreds of miles of territory wholly strange to them, organised them, taught them, interceded for them. Now, thanks to him, they had their freedom, their laws, their worship. One thing only was lacking, a territory of their own, and there it lay in front of them. But not for him!

How comely to the yearning eyes of Moses that vision of Canaan, how heartrendingly elusive! On another mountain, in another age, not God, but Satan, will offer to the young eyes of Moses' successor, a prospect still more spellbinding, still more illusory, of 'all the kingdoms of the world and the glory of them'. These visions are based on the ancient, very sensible, legal practice of both parties to a transfer of land, taking a joint survey of the territory to be transferred. God was making over Canaan to the Sons of Israel in the person of Moses. Satan will deceitfully offer to surrender the world for a simple act of worship. The survey takes place for Moses at the very end of his assignment; with Christ, at the beginning. Moses has already won his people their freedom, taught them the Law of Yahweh and shown them the way into the Land of the Promise.

Christ will have yet to redeem the world, promulgate the New Law and bring mankind to the Kingdom of God. Moses is not to enter the land, but to lay down his life at its margin. Christ will certainly enter his kingdom, but he will be close to death when he says, "Today you will be with me in Paradise".

Moses will die outside of Canaan, according to some texts because he had twice struck the rock to bring water from it, when he had been instructed merely to address it. However, in two places in Deuteronomy Moses says of his exclusion from Canaan, 'The Lord was angry with me on your account'. Culpably or otherwise, he has become involved in Israel's lack of faith, and so must share the common fate of all members of his own doubting generation. Christ's generation will also fail in faith, refusing to believe in him and sending him to his death.

It will be in terms of Moses that Matthew will present Christ to contemporary Judaism. For a present day Christian it is instructive to look at Moses in terms of Christ. We can have too Olympian a notion of Moses. We associate him with the thunders and lightnings of Sinai until we almost credit him with launching them. Does not Michelangelo's Moses suggest a Jewish Jove the Thunderer? Moses is not for the most part a dominating figure. The baby crying in his basket among the river reeds, the stateless refugee in Midian, terrified out of his wits to be told, 'I will send you to Pharaoh', the leader begging to lead no more, the old man who must die just as his life's work is about to reach its consummaton, none of these are figures of power. Moses is highly vulnerable, exposed, his life poured out for his people. Michelangelo's Moses misleads. Think rather of his Pieta.

# Jonathan's Love

*'If I say to the lad, 'Look, the arrows are on this side of you, take them', then you are to come, for . . . it is safe for you and there is no danger. But if I say to the youth, 'Look, the arrows are beyond you', then go'. (I Sam 20.21,2)*

Were it not for the uncontemporary arrows, one might be in a Le Carre novel with two of Smiley's people arranging 'safety procedures' for a rendezvous unknown to 'the opposition'. The story is somewhat older. The setting is Palestine three thousand years ago; 'the opposition' supplying the atmosphere of menace is King Saul; the man addressed is David, and the one setting up the meeting with its Sarratt precautions is Saul's eldest son, Jonathan.

Jonathan is, by my reckoning, one of the nicest people in the Old Testament, though I am forced to grant that the competition is limited, the folk in the Old Testament being generally awesome rather than engaging. Jonathan makes a sudden appearance in the First Book of Samuel: already a successful commander against the Philistines, dashing, courageous and so popular that when his life is forfeit because of an unwitting breach of a fierce one-day taboo decreed by Saul, the people protect him, 'there shall not one hair of his head fall to the ground', and then ransom him. By birth, by prowess, in popular esteem this is plainly Saul's heir.

Then there enters upon the scene, with the light springing tread of the shepherd lad, but encumbered by the bulky trophy of Goliath's severed head, one of literature's most brilliant heroes: David, son of Jesse. Nobody gives him a more appreciative reception than Jonathan. 'Jonathan loved him as his own soul . . . stripped himself of the robe that was upon him and gave it to David, and his armour, and even his sword and his bow and his girdle'. Soon David's successes in war and reputation eclipse those of Jonathan and even of Saul. 'Saul has slain his thousands and David his tens of thousands', sing the women. 'What more can he have', comments the morose, but alert, Saul, 'but the Kingdom?'

Jonathan in contrast is wholly without jealousy. He 'delighted much in David'. He defends him to Saul's face, once successfully, later unsuccessfully. 'For as long as the son of Jesse lives', the furious King declares, 'neither you nor your kingdom shall be established'. Quite impervious to this appeal to his self-interest Jonathan persists in urging David's innocence until the King, exasperated beyond bearing by such blindness to their common interest, attacks him with his spear.

'And Jonathan rose from table in fierce anger and ate no food . . . for he was grieving for David'. No hint, notice, of fear for his own safety. It is on the following day that Jonathan goes to his clandestine meeting with David. David, to do him justice, on this occasion matches Jonathan's devotion with his own. His rapidly blossoming career at court is at an end; he must abandon wife and home, and will be lucky to keep his life, yet at this moment his heart has room only for Jonathan and his grief at their parting. 'And as soon as the lad had gone, David rose from beside the stone heap and fell on his face to the ground, and bowed three times; and they kissed one another and wept with one another until David recovered himself'.

There follows one of the most thrilling sections of the David saga, his guerilla period, in which at the head of his kinsmen (whose lives were forfeit with his own) and a group of outcasts, he survives by constantly moving, exchanging remote refuges for the inhospitable wilderness to evade Saul's determined pursuit.

At times, in spite of his natural guile and his acquired fighting skills, his moral wears thin. At one such period Jonathan makes his way to him. 'And David was afraid because Saul had come out to seek his life . . . and Jonathan rose and went to David at Horesh and strengthened his hand in God. And he said to him, "Fear not, for the hand of Saul, my father, shall not find you; you shall be king over Israel and I shall be next to you" . . . and the two of them made a covenant before the Lord'. Saul, fiercely protective of his kingship, hunts David whenever the task of holding off the Philistines lets him. His eldest son travels the same road only to hearten David and waive his own claim to the succession in favour of a desperate fugitive.

It was the last meeting and their last parting. The Philistines had gathered for a major onslaught. Saul, depressive and obsessive, but always a king, went forth to meet them, and Jonathan loyally accompanied him to share his defeat and death on Mount Gilboa. That life which had promised so much when he was a gallant young captain and popular heir to the throne ended without his ever being King, having become partly estranged from his father, widely separated from his beloved friend and in circumstances of overwhelming defeat. (Homework: Compare Gilboa with Calvary.)

Yet, if we want to know how to love God, and how to love our 'neighbour' we might learn much from Jonathan's life and death. Note his generous appreciation of David's qualities, how he 'stripped himself' to enrich David; how he 'delighted in him'. (How much it would do for you if someone 'delighted in you'); how he risks his father's anger and even his own life; how readily he accepts second place ('He must increase and I must decrease'). More than once I have been asked by someone I was trying to help, 'Do I mean anything to you, or is this your Christian charity?' Worse, I once had a superior, who, if he found a room chilly, would say, 'It's as cold as charity'. David's final word on Jonathan was 'your love to me was wonderful, passing the love of women'. I suggest one could revivify one's whole understanding and exercise of 'charity' by admiring Jonathan. I told you he was nice!

# 'Once More the Godlike David'

*And the Lord struck the child that Uriah's wife bore to David, and it became sick. David besought God for the child; and David fasted and went in and lay all night upon the ground. And the elders of his house stood beside him to raise him from the ground; but he would not, nor did he eat food with them. On the seventh day the child died.*

*(2 Sam 12. 15-17)*

When Dryden used the epithet 'godlike', albeit with the tongue bucally situated, he was writing to flatter Charles, King of England, rather than to pay tribute to David, King of Israel. The Scripture is less fulsome, but still credits David with an astounding array of gifts. Its first description of him runs: 'he was ruddy and had beautiful eyes and was handsome'. The second: 'Behold, I have seen a son of Jesse the Bethlehemite, who is skilful in playing, a man of valour, a man of war, prudent in speech, and a man of good presence: and the Lord is with him'.

As a recommendation for the post of court minstrel to King Saul this list of attributes makes him sound somewhat overqualified, but in the course of his career David was to justify every word of it. With his lyre he charmed away Saul's black moods. With only his sling he faced and felled the heavily armed Goliath. In war he proved himself at every level, whether leading Saul's men in raids against the Philistines, captaining a band of outlaws and free-booters, or as king carrying war into the territories of Israel's former enemies, subduing them and laying them under tribute. In his zigzag ascent to the throne he showed himself 'prudent' in more than speech. If at times authority seems to drop into his lap, it is because he has made himself the right man in the right place at the right time with the right resources, who has said and done the right things. That he had been in so many tight situations, that he had survived very much against the odds, and always in the end come out on top, was clear proof to Hebrews that 'Jahweh was with him'.

Of his greatest asset Saul's informant had made no mention. When David entered Saul's service, 'Saul loved him greatly'. Saul's son Jonathan 'loved him as his own soul', and 'Saul's daughter Michal loved David'. The women of Israel celebrated him in a calypso: 'Saul has slain his thousands, and David his tens of thousands' which turned Saul's love into morbid jealousy. When David the leader of outlaws said, 'O that someone would give me water to drink from the well of Bethlehem!', then 'three mighty men broke through the camp of the Philistines, and drew water out of the well of Bethlehem . . . and brought it to David'. With this ability to inspire devotion in both men and women, in his peers and in his followers, and with his outstanding ability to read a military or political situation, David was well equipped to 'achieve greatness', especially so when 'Jahweh was with him'.

There is nothing 'godlike' about David of the scene from 2 Samuel quoted above, where he lies face to the ground, foodless and distraught, pleading for the life of his sick child. Now his musical talent, his proven courage, his personal magnetism, his political sagacity avail nothing. Here he is alone, although surrounded by solicitous kinsmen, for what do they care if Bathsheba's child lives or dies? He hugs the earth like the captured citizen of a fallen city before its conqueror hoping his life will be spared. And the Lord, who has been 'with him' from boyhood, now proves pitiless.

With his many-sided brilliance in eclipse, one aspect of David stands out the more. It is that capacity not always highly developed in the charming and successful, the ability to love, and to love to distraction. David is not storming Heaven for an only son. There must have been enough royal sons in his polygamous household to field an infant rugby team, and it would have been sadly common for Death to dismiss one from the field. Why was this babe so precious, expecially as it had been begotten in discreditable adultery with Bathsheba while her husband fought in David's wars? David had tried to pass this child off as Uriah's boy by summoning him home to Jerusalem. When the ruse failed because of Uriah's loyal refusal to sleep at home while 'my lord Joab and the servants of my lord are camping in the open field', David, now desperate, had sent him back to Joab with sealed instructions; 'Set Uriah in the forefront of the hardest fighting, and then draw back from him . . . that he may be struck down and die'. The advent of the child, then, is intimately associated with David's moral disintegration into an adulterer, into the murder by treachery of an upright and brave servant. Yet David begs that the child will be spared.

He has been left in no doubt that he has forfeited the favour of the God who had prohibited adultery, forbidden murder and who always kept faith. He is to be punished in his dynasty, 'now therefore the sword shall never depart from your house'; in his personal male honour, 'I will take your wives before your eyes and give them to your neighbour'; and finally, 'the child that is born to you shall die'. David appeals only on one point. He 'besought God for the child' whose conception had set in train the whole debacle.

In later years another son, Absolom, will seize the kingship, take Jerusalem, violate David's concubines and pursue David intending, no doubt, to kill him. In the ensuing battle David will have a single preoccupation, 'Is the young man Absolom safe?' Nor is it only to his sons that David's love goes out. He has returned Jonathan's love 'passing the love of women'. He certainly loved Bathsheba. He had first sent for her to indulge in carnal lust, but it was surely to protect her rather than himself, that he had recalled Uriah, and so started on the downward path of deceit, betrayal and murder. To Bathsheba's second son he will bequeath the kingdom.

I said that there is nothing 'godlike' about the prostrate, imploring David. Yet, is there any human quality so Godlike as self-disregarding love? Am I justified in seeing a more than superficial resemblance between this scene and that separated from it in time by a thousand years, and in space less than a mile, at Gethsemene, where the 'Son of David' 'greatly distressed and troubled', fell on the ground and prayed 'remove this cup from me'?

# Tribute to Jezebel

*When Jehu came to Jezreel, Jezebel heard of it; and she painted her eyes, and adorned her head and looked out of the window. (2 Kings 9.30).*

The *femme fatale*, her weaponry all honed and burnished, ready to essay the conquest of yet another male? Far from it! This is an old woman, who, coolly aware that she is about to be murdered, has been at some pains to make herself presentable for this not unimportant occasion. An old woman, but a great lady, daughter of a king, widow of a king, mother and grandmother of kings, a princess of the Phoenicians.

'The Phoenicians', wrote Pomponius Mela, a thousand years later, 'were a clever race, who prospered in war and peace'. Clever they certainly were as agriculturalists, shipwrights, sailors and traders. The Mediterranean bristled with their trading posts and colonies, Carthage, the most successful, being founded by Dido, a great-niece of Jezebel. Phoenician sailors are thought to have circumnavigated Africa, and even to have sighted the remote island of Albion. The Phoenicians produced builders, weavers, dyers of distinction and talented artists in metal and ivory. Solomon owed his temple to their craftsmen; we are largely indebted to their scribes for our alphabet.

Jezebel, daughter of Ethbaal, King of Tyre, was married to Ahab, King of Israel. Ahab seems to have been a competent military organiser, but bafflingly ambivalent in the religious and moral sphere. Jezebel, on the other hand, promoted the cause of her ancestral gods with Phoenician clarity of purpose and resoluteness of action, maintaining a small army of prophets of Baal and executing the prophets of Jahweh. Elijah was forced to hide beyond the Jordan and later beyond the northern border. Thence he emerged to beard Ahab and demand a confrontation with the prophets of Baal and Asherah. 'Is it you, you troubler of Israel?', was Ahab's greeting. Ahab's exasperated tolerance of Elijah reminds one of Herod Antipas with John the Baptist, both rulers caught squirming between an uncompromising man of God and a ruthless spouse. Elijah got his confrontation, won it hands down with fire from heaven and, as a triumphant coda, massacred the pagan prophets.

Ahab let it all happen; Jezebel reacted very differently. She sent Elijah a message swearing she would dispatch him after her own prophets within twenty-four hours. It seems rather sporting of her to give him fair warning. Elijah took advantage of it to fly to Judah. There in the wilderness he was minded to give Jezebel best and resign from the conflict. 'It is enough, now, O Lord, take away my life'.

There was nothing sporting about Jezebel's dealing with Naboth of Jezreel. Finding Ahab literally prostrate with frustration at Naboth's refusal to sell his ancestral vineyard she quite outdoes Lady Macbeth. Taking the entire matter into her own efficiently amoral hands she used the royal seal and had Naboth framed for blasphemy and duly stoned to death. A restored Ahab happily took possession of the vineyard and found himself confronted by a revived Elijah. 'Have you found me, O my enemy?', Ahab resignedly asked, only to be told in the most downright fashion of the retribution awaiting himself and Jezebel and of the coming extinction of his dynasty. Ahab, with surprising docility, repented publicly in sackcloth. That enigmatic King would meet his end in battle. A stray arrow found a gap in his armour, and he slowly bled to death, propped up in the chariot, his face to the enemy. The narrator is careful to tell us that when the chariot was washed 'the dogs licked up the blood and the harlots washed in it'. Yet any Hebrew must have considered it to Ahab's credit that he died discharging the primary duty of a king, 'to go out before us and fight our battles'.

It was another eight years before Elijah's predictions were fully realised. Jehu, a chariot commander, led a military coup in which he shot King Joram of Israel with his own bow, while Joram's nephew, the King of Judah, was mortally wounded. Apprised of the fate of son and grandson, the aged Jezebel did not attempt flight, but, as we have seen, arrayed herself to meet their killer face to face, upstaging him from her window. On his arrival she precludes all possibility of his sparing or ignoring her, meeting him with insult, her verbal shafts as telling as Jehu's own arrows. 'You Zimri, (Zimri, another chariot commander, forty years before, had killed his king, been repudiated by the army and committed suicide within the week) murderer of your master!' Jehu cannot overlook the words or their implications. She is toppled from her window, trampled by his horses and her corpse dismembered by scavenging dogs.

Did the author feel any compassion or admiration for this woman who died every bit as gamely as her husband? I think not. For him she was an idolatress and a murderess, who had corrupted Israel's King, who had come close to perverting the whole nation, who had nearly eradicated the worship of the God of Israel in favour of lascivious heathen cults. The last minutes of her life were given to proudly defying Jehu. Her entire queenship had been one long insolent challenge to Jahweh.

In my eyes, Jezebel does all the wrong things, but in the right way. Unlike her husband she is totally committed. A Phoenician to the tips of her bejewelled fingers, she pursues her objectives with vigour, courage, ingenuity and a touch of style. 'You shall love the Lord your God with all your heart, and with all your soul, and with all your might'. When it comes to the 'how' of things Jezebel, Moses and Jesus are at one. Then commit your every resource, serve God with all your strength, with whatever courage you can muster, with all your ingenuity, and, if possible, with panache.

# Elijah's Despair

*But he himself went a day's journey into the wilderness,
and came and sat down under a broom tree; and he asked that
he might die, saying, 'It is enough, now, O Lord, take away
my life; for I am no better than my fathers', (I Kings 19,4).*

To a connoisseur of discouragement like myself, a despairing Old Testament Hebrew is of special interest. To be so overwhelmed by his own inadequacy in the face of the world, that he yearns for the termless desolation of Sheol, a man must be hopeless indeed. Here by interest is all the greater, because the demoralised individual is an Old Testament figure of the very first rank, the prophet Elijah.

There is no hint of diffidence, never mind demoralisation, about Elijah's irruption on the biblical scene. He does irrupt. We are told nothing of his early life, or of his previous history, if any, as a prophet. Israel was at that time ruled over by Ahab, who 'did more to provoke the Lord God of Israel than all the kings of Israel before him'. He worshipped Baal, and allowed his fascinating and ruthless consort, Jezebel, to execute the 'prophets of the Lord'. To Ahab Elijah boldly declared, 'there shall be neither dew nor rain these years, except by my word'. The clang of the down-flung gauntlet rings in the phrase 'except by my word', for to give rain was the prerogative of Baal, 'who mounts the clouds', of whom a Ugaritic hymn declares:

> Baal will send abundance of rain,
> Abundance of moisture with snow.

There was no rain, and while the land withered, Elijah took refuge, first beyond the Jordan, where he was fed by Arabs (probably not 'ravens'), and then in Jezebel's home territory, with a widow whose jar of meal and cruise of oil proved inexhaustible. The widow's son came close to death, and Elijah seems to blame himself for attracting disaster. 'O Lord, my God, hast thou brought calamity even upon the widow with whom I sojourn?' A strange attitude when God had provided for him among kindly gentiles, and with an unfailing supply of food! Was he thinking of his fellow prophets slain by Jezebel? Or of the parched soil of Israel? He begged for the life of the child, who did revive.

Elijah beards Ahab once more, this time demanding a confrontation with 'the four hundred and fifty prophets of Baal and the four hundred prophets of Asherah' to take place at Mount Carmel before 'all Israel'. There is no diffidence here, nor at the subsequent encounter, where he allowed his heathen rivals some hours of strenuous, but vain, intercession, before drenching his own offering and altar, and then calling upon God to ignite them. The offering was promptly consumed by fire, the people powerfully impressed, and the victory consummated by the slaughter of the pagan prophets and the coming of 'a great rain'. This resounding triumph proves far from complete. The redoubtable Jezebel fights back, compelling Elijah to flee to the wilderness of Juda. Here discouragement floods his soul. Carmel has changed nothing. Ahab remains ambivalent, Jezebel relentless, the people acquiescent. So Elijah asks that he might die. Once more miraculously sustained, he tramps to 'Horeb, the Mount of God', still without hope. 'I, even I only, am left: and they seek my life to take it away'.

Is Elijah's mistake that he focusses on himself? At Zarephath he blames himself for bringing death to the widow's house. In the wilderness he says, 'I am no better than my fathers'. At Horeb, 'I only am left'. Is Jahweh powerless because Elijah is no better than his fathers? Did it matter on Carmel that there were eight hundred and fifty pagan prophets, and Elijah, only Elijah, for Jahweh? Had God not shown that He could preserve Elijah's life, even among the gentiles? Was the power that had humbled Egypt nullified by Ahab's neglect, or Jezebel's defiance, or Israel's defection?

Here the Procrustean exigencies of this page require a drastic compression, not to say truncation of the Elijah story.

At Horeb he was instructed to anoint Jehu to be King in place of Ahab, and to provide for the continuity of his own mission by enrolling Elisha. He did the second, and Elisha later procured the anointing of Jehu. When Jezebel obtained Naboth's vineyard for Ahab by an impious travesty of justice, it was Elijah who delivered the divine rebuke and announced the divine retribution, doing so to such effect that Ahab performed public penance. The measure of Israel's later respect for Elijah is to be gauged from the story that he was taken 'up to heaven by a whirlwind'. Elisha who was persistently dogging his footsteps, found himself separated from Elijah by 'a chariot of fire and horses of fire'. Fire, of course, is a symbol of the divine presence, while the chariot, so fearsome in war, perhaps indicates the powerful protection extended to Elijah. It is not the fiery chariot which is most significant, but the unique ending — if it is an ending — of Elijah's life. The greatest figures in Hebrew history, Abraham, Jacob, Moses and David had, without exception, died and been buried, gone, in David's words, 'the way of all the earth', which led presumably to Sheol. Elijah was taken 'up to heaven', and his body was nowhere to be found.

There developed a conviction that Elijah would come again before 'the day of the Lord'. This is stated in the last two verses of Malachi, and is therefore the final message of the Old Testament. This expectation of Elijah's reappearance is very obvious in the Gospels, where the figure of John the Baptist is plainly modelled on him. John wears the 'garment of haircloth with a girdle of leather'; he emerges from the wilderness of Judaea with the word of God, and incurs the fatal hostility of a royal lady. The crowning testimony to the importance of Elijah is in his appearance at the Transfiguration, where Moses and he — and Mark plus Elijah first — sum up the whole of the revelation of the Old Testament as witnessing to the Messiah of the New.

Is it not worth noting that when Elijah, peer of Moses, focusses on himself, he is without hope; that when he devotes himself to delivering the message of God, he carries himself fearlessly?

# Let Us Rise Up
# and Build

*And the king said to me, 'Why is your face sad, seeing you are not sick?' . . . Then I was very much afraid. I said to the king, 'Let the king live for ever! Why should not my face be sad, when the city, the place of my fathers' sepulchres, lies waste, and its gates have been destroyed by fire?' (Nehemiah 2.3.)*

I had not appreciated until I became interested in Nehemiah just how vast the Persian Empire was. It stretched from Kashmir in the east to the frontiers of Greece in the west; it reached northward to the shores of the Aral Sea and south to the borders of Ethiopia. At the centre of that Empire, in the heart of the palace, Nehemiah served the king himself. The affairs of that immense empire were transacted in his immediate neighbourhood; intrigue, intricate and incessant, must have been part of the atmosphere he breathed; elaborate spectacle imposing architecture, rich artefacts formed his setting. There, midst that luxurious, cosmopolitan environment, where there was everything to interest, absorb and fascinate, the mind of Nehemiah was hundreds of miles away, focussed upon an unprosperous, politically insignificant corner of a far province, where a decayed capital partly stood, partly lay in ruins.

Almost a century and a half before, a Babylonian general had come to Jerusalem. 'He burned the house of the Lord, and the king's house, and all the houses.' He also 'broke down the walls around Jerusalem' and carried its citizens into exile, but 'left some of the poorest of the land to be vinedressers and ploughmen.' The city and the countryside were then further pillaged by the neighbouring Edomites, intent upon both plunder and revenge. After fifty years of exile, when the more benevolent Persians had replaced the Babylonians, a number of Jews were allowed, even encouraged to return, and to rebuild the Temple. The problems of resettlement and restoration were grave. Leadership, authority and inspiration were too intermittent; the hostile factors too powerful to allow the revived community to do much more than survive.

It was this city, although he had probably never seen it, and this community, whose traditional taboos declared a eunuch like himself to be unfit to belong to it, which so preoccupied Nehemiah. Told that its citizens were 'in great trouble and shame', he 'sat down and wept, and mourned for days.' How long it took him to decide that he himself must assume responsibility for the wellbeing of Jerusalem, he does not say. It was certainly three months or more before he let his distress be seen by the king. Taking a considerable risk, he confided in the king, whose own provincial officials could well have been responsibile for Jerusalem's recent distress. He succeeded in winning, not only leave of absence, but the authority and the materials to rebuild Jerusalem. So Nehemiah, the royal cupbearer, rode more than a thousand miles along the highway which linked Susa with Egypt, into what was, despite his Jewish blood and his religious fidelity, a largely alien world.

In Jerusalem he said nothing of his plans. On his third night there, he rode quietly out of the city, with his attendance on foot, and made his own survey of the shattered walls. In the palace at Susa he had dreamed of rebuilding these walls. He had come a thousand miles to do so. He has now opened his campaign, not with an eloquent appeal to national pride and civic self-interest, but with a yard by yard inspection of the wall's actual condition. This is an authentic rebuilder. He starts by facing facts. Then will come the moving address, and after that the sincere response, 'Let us rise up and build.'

And there were other facts for Nehemiah to face, most of them more intractable than tumbled masonry and wrecked gates. Local officials threatened to accuse him of preparing rebellion. Nehemiah ignored them, relying perhaps on his royal commission and his own superior experience of the workings of the court. When he learned that they were preparing a direct assault upon the city in concert with 'the Arabs and the Ammonites and the Ashdodites' he took the threat very seriously indeed. His concern to provide an effective defence without halting the work of reconstruction is proverbial: 'half of my servants worked on the construction and half held the spears, shields, bows and coats of mail'. The labourer 'with one hand laboured on the work and with the other held his weapon. And each of the builders had his sword girded at his side while he built.'

The gravest threat was internal. Bad harvests had forced the poorer people to mortgage their fields, vineyards and houses to the rich. When the latter foreclosed, their victims found themselves reduced to selling their children in order to survive. Nehemiah summoned the nobles and the officials and tore into them with such effect that they promised to return everything, and even to forego their interest. One suspects that this wholesale Zachaeus-like conversion sprang less from remorse than from a salutary fear of Nehemiah. When it came to compelling this community 'to walk in the fear of God', Nehemiah did not hesitate. On this occasion he 'took an oath of them to do as they promised.' He stopped them trading on the sabbath by keeping the city gates closed the whole day, and forbidding traders to come anywhere near the city during it. 'If you do so again I will lay hands on you.' Even the most authoritarian of parish priests would hesitate to employ his method of discouraging mixed marriages. 'I contended with them and cursed them and beat some of them and pulled out their hair.'

The wall was rebuilt, all two miles and more of it. It was dedicated with splended ceremonies, in the organisation of which the Persian court official must for once have felt at home. 'And the joy of Jerusalem was heard afar off.' He was rebuilding more than walls. He was reconstructing a nation. He looked to their unity, trying to prevent one section from exploiting another. He tried to maintain their separateness by, admittedly, rather rough methods. Above all, he was concerned for their unique relationship with God. Hence his emphasis on the rigorous observance of the sabbath and his meticulous provision for the temple ritual, and still more his care that this people be fully aware of, and wholeheartedly reaffirm, their covenant with 'the Lord, the great God.'

There is always so much rebuilding to do in the world, in the Church and in our own lives. Has perhaps the edifice of my prayer become as dilapidated as the walls of Jerusalem? 'We have sometimes', said a wise lady to me, 'to begin by rebuilding our morale to rebuild.' You may be helped by the example of Nehemiah, the imperial cupbearer, making his slow way across the Judaean hillside, tracing in the moonlight those furlongs of fallen stones.

# Jonah's Psalm

*Now the word of the Lord came to Jonah, the son of Amitai, saying, 'Arise, go to Nineveh, that great city, and cry out against it; for their wickedness has come up before me'. But Jonah rose to flee to Tarshish from the presence of the Lord. (Jon 1.1-3)*

Some time ago I went to the Nineveh Room in the British Museum to look at the stone reliefs. They show sturdy Assyrian warriors in confident assault on high-walled cities, then grimly triumphant, callously depositing the severed heads of the vanquished defenders in grisly heaps at the feet of an unruffled scribe, who dispassionately records the score. Elsewhere equally formidable overseers direct the slave gangs, which toil uphill with large baskets of new quarried stone, or strain to move massive monuments into place. Jonah needed no pictures. The bloody tide of Assyrian conquest had drowned all Northern Israel, swamping its cities, carrying its inhabitants into exile and even lapping menacingly at the walls of Jerusalem. And these are the people Jonah had been told to denounce to their faces, and in their own capital! Nineveh lay overland to the North East. Jonah took a ship sailing due West, and who shall blame him?

My first surprise was to realise that Jonah is not at all timid. 'There was a mighty tempest on the sea, so that the ship threatened to break up'. The sailors are terrified. They jettison their cargo and beseech their gods. Meanwhile, to the indignation of the captain, the landsman, Jonah, is placidly asleep. When the lots are cast and point to Jonah as the cause of the storm, he openly admits responsibility, and calmly urges the crew to save themselves by throwing him after the cargo. They hesitate (it is another of the book's surprises that while Jonah, the Hebrew, is constantly at odds with God, the gentiles never behave less than well). Only when they have again tried and failed to bring the boat to land, do they accept his offer and toss him to the waves.

Everyone knows about the great fish which swallowed Jonah, which swam with him in its belly for three days, to regurgitate him on the shore, alive and well. Few people, more's the pity, know the psalm, reverberating with confidence and gratitude, which Jonah is credited with composing during this Mediterranean cruise. Whether it was this access of confidence which braced him to obey the second command and to go to Nineveh, I cannot tell. It may merely have been a resigned recognition that 'the Lord, the God of Heaven, and the dry land', for so he had described his God to the sailors, was not to be evaded anywhere. He went to Nineveh and proclaimed, 'Yet forty days and Nineveh shall be overthrown'. The result is far more incredible than the story of the fish. The Ninevites, who have destroyed dynasties and uprooted whole nations, listen to this solitary Hebrew, believe and do penance. The King orders fasting, sackcloth and prayer and real conversion, 'let everyone turn from his evil way and from the violence which is in his hands'. And God spares him.

Never was a preacher so utterly successful as Jonah was. And even the least successful could not have been more unhappy about it. 'But it displeased Jonah exceedingly, and he was angry . . . That is why I made haste to Tarshish; for I knew that thou art a gracious God and merciful, slow to anger, and abounding in steadfast love, and repentant of evil'. I blink at the ingenious perversity by which that list of attributes is made to sound like an accusation, and is then used to justify the plea, 'take my life from me . . . it is better for me to die than to live'. The Christian must bear in mind that Jonah is not asking to go to Heaven ahead of his time; a Hebrew saw this life as followed by the blankness of Sheol, and it is that condition which Jonah finds preferable to going on living. Why? Was it because God had compelled him to announce a punishment which was then cancelled, which he had known would be cancelled? Or did he believe that the Assyrians ought to have been destroyed in return for the destruction they had meted out to others, especially, of course, to Israel?

Jonah went out of the city and there squatted, not unlike Diogenes in his tub, in a 'booth', a DIY construction of vegetation, which kept off the worst of the blistering sun. 'God appointed a plant' which sprang up and gave additional shade. 'Jonah was exceedingly glad because of the plant'. But the next day the plant withered and a 'sultry east wind' blew and Jonah's spirits plummetted yet again . . . 'and he asked that he might die'. In another of his frank dialogues with God he insists that his despair, caused by the death of the plant, is justified. 'I do well to be angry, angry enough to die'. God, of course, has the last word, 'You pity the plant . . . and should not I pity Nineveh . . . in which there are a hundred and twenty thousand persons who do not know their right hand from their left?'

The message of the Book of Jonah seems clear enough. 'Thou art a gracious God and merciful . . . and abounding in steadfast love', a love which reaches out even at the unspeakable Assyrians. Yet as a practising melancholic I am fascinated by the personality of Jonah. This is a pessimist's pessimist. In the space of four short chapters he thrice asks to die. He can regard God's 'steadfast love' as a basic fact, apparently without deriving the slightest comfort therefrom; can even, as I indicated above, seem to make it a matter of complaint. at the moment when he has been most effective, he is thoroughly dejected. He can face death unflinchingly, and is quite demoralised by the extinction of his (God's) plant. The gentile sailors are humane and the Assyrians receptive, but he seems to maintain himself in disgruntled isolation from them, and even, in a sense, from God's steadfast love. Is there any lesson here for pessimists? That God finds us more intractable than the Assyrians? Perhaps we ought to have more frequent recourse to Jonah's psalm in the second chapter, 'I called to the Lord, out of my distress, and he answered me'.

# Judith of Jewry

*Then Judith came and lay down, and Holofernes' heart
was ravished with her and he was moved with a great desire
to possess her; . . . So Holofernes said to her, 'Drink now,
and be merry with us!' Judith said, 'I will drink now, my
lord, because my life means more to me today than in all
the days since I was born.' (Judith 12.16)*

I should love to see two first rate actors playing this scene.
What expression should Holofernes wear at this moment? A
complacent smirk would be beneath the dignity of a battle-
hardened Commander-in-Chief of the Imperial Armies, who
received deference and obedience from his men, and the flattery
of capitulating cities and yielding women, all as a matter of
course. Yet he should show some satisfaction that a campaign,
which had so far been an unqualified success, would shortly
advance a further stage with the surrender of Bethulia, leaving
the road open to the subjugation of all Judaea and the plunder
of Jerusalem, a victory deliciously symbolised in anticipation
by his effortless conquest of this magnificent woman. The part
of Judith sets an even stiffer test with those words, 'my life
means more to me today than in all the days since I was born.'
How is the actress to suggest the fierce double entendre of a
woman appearing to savour in advance the embraces of a godlike lover, when she is actually steeling herself to be his one
successful opponent, his final, fatal adversary, his assassin?

The story brims over with cinematic material, the gathering
of Holofernes' great army, his triumphant march by mountain
and plain and the broken cities and burning harvests in his
wake. It should not be difficult to present the growing conster-
nation of Jerusalem, a city lately rebuilt, as Holofernes' tri-

umphs bring closer and closer the prospect of a second destruction of Zion, and the second desecration of its Temple. The messengers could be shown spurring to all the Israelite cities of the North, with the consequent manning of the hilltops, and the purposeful occupation of the mountain passes. How satisfactorily tension would mount as Holofernes' army comes in sight, and the whole cavalry force is paraded before the key Israelite city of Bethulia! The alarmed Israelites kindle the fires on their watchtowers and stand by their weapons all night long, precautions which, disastrously, do nothing at all to prevent the army cutting off their only source of water.

Yet a cinema audience could not be expected to realise that Nebuchadnezzar, the name of Holofernes' King, is the name of the Babylonian King who had destroyed Jerusalem and deported the Jews, that in this story he is made King of Assyria, so that Israel's two most powerful enemies are represented together in one person. Similarly, Holofernes' army is made to contain Moabites, Ammonites, Canaanites and Edomites to broaden this irresistible combination of traditional foes. It also requires some knowledge of Jewish history to realise how brittle would be the confidence of the Jews so recently returned from their deportation, how frail their hopes of withstanding such a combination of enemies. As Holofernes demanded that 'all nations should worship Nebuchadnezzar only', the Israelites face the likelihood not only of defeat, conquest and slavery, but also of the extinction of the worship of Jahweh. Their only hope is that Holofernes might be held in the narrow passes, where his numerical superiority would be neutralised, and his cavalry unusable. The key to the passes is the — apparently invented — city of Bethulia. Bethulia is prepared and resolute, until Holofernes, by the advice of his local auxiliaries, severs its water supply. The citizens decide they will hold out a further five days and then surrender. Five days stand between them and a capitulation which will entail the conquest of Jerusalem and the political and religious extinction of Israel, five days . . . and a woman!

But what a woman! 'She was very beautiful in appearance'. She well knew how to array herself 'in all her woman's finery', gown, tiara and abundant jewelry, so as 'to make herself very beautiful, to entice the eyes of all men who might see her,' her speech, whether she is addressing the Jewish elders, an Assyrian patrol or the great Holofernes, casts as strong a spell as her looks. 'There is not such a woman from one end of the earth to the other, either for beauty of face or wisdom of speech.' Her virtues shine even more brilliantly than her jewelry. A childless widow, she has lived austerely and devoutly. 'No one spoke ill of her.' Her observance of The Law is so exact that even to the Assyrian camp she takes her own supply of kosher food, and will eat nothing else. She alone in Bethulia possesses an unconditional confidence in God. Her address to the elders is a superb statement of Jewish faith. It seems to me to begin where 'Job' finishes. This woman is a combination of Helen of Troy, Joan of Arc and Catherine of Sienna with a quicksilver quality all her own.

So Holofernes' corpse comes to lie bleeding beside his bed, the corpse headless and the bed stripped of its canopy. As David had borne Goliath's head from the field, so Judith and her maid bring their trophy and the gem-encrusted canopy back to Bethulia in their foodbag. The reanimated Israelites rout the leaderless Assyrian army and Israel, its capital and its worship are saved. Judith, I am sorry to say, is not a historical personage. Neither is the Good Samaritan, but we hold him in admiration and try to gain inspiration from him. Are you disedified that Judith wields her sex-appeal to bring down Holofernes? David overcame his adversary with his sling, the only weapon a stripling shepherd could manage. Judith, by the same principle, 'undid him with the beauty of her countenance.' Judith in Holofernes' camp, elegant, eloquent, resplendent is a memorable figure. Judith in Bethulia, when hope has dried up with the water supply, is more splendid still. This woman's mind, heart and life are focussed, unshakeably focussed, on God. She can handle clothes, jewelry, words and certainly men, but to one clear end. Her commitment and her hope is unflawed. At Bethulia's worst moment she says, 'In spite of everything let us give thanks to the Lord our God, who is putting us to the test.' 'Thanks', mind you!

# 'En un Mot, Elle est Femme'

*The daughter of Pharaoh . . . saw the basket among the reeds and sent her maid to fetch it. When she opened it she saw the child; and the babe was crying. She took pity on him . . .*

*(Exodus 2.5,6)*

At that moment the Egyptian princess became a member of a conspiracy of women. It included the Hebrew midwives who had evaded the Pharaoh's genocidal decree, the anonymous mother who had hidden her babe for three months and the sister anxiously watching on the river bank. With a royal protectress the success of the association was assured, and Moses survived to confront Pharaoh, to unleash the plagues on Egypt, to lead the Israelites to freedom, to keep that wayward and stiff-necked people together and on the move to their Promised Land. When Moses came striding down from Sinai, clasping the stone tablets of the Law, 'Aaron and all the people' dared not look on the face which the princess had once seen puckered in a baby's helpless distress, at a moment when the whole future of Israel had depended on a woman's compassion.

There are other occasions in Hebrew literature when the survival of their nation is made to depend on a woman. In the Book of Esther, Haman, anticipating another final solution by two and a half millenia, persuades King Ahasuerus 'to destroy, to slay and to annihilate, all Jews, young and old, women and children, in one day', and this 'from India to Ethiopia'. Unknown to Haman, the Queen herself is a Jewess, who has hitherto 'not made known her people or her kindred'. Shall she intercede? If she does, will she not expose her own life to the penalties of the decree? And how to intercede when to enter the inner court unsummoned by the King was to commit an offence punishable by death? Esther's decision: 'I will go to the King, though it is against the law; and if I perish, I perish'. In full queenly tenue she proceeds unbidden to the inner court, is pardoned for her intrusion and does not immediately plead for the lives of her people, but makes the opening move in a deadly game of Courtier's Chess. So adroitly does she move that Haman finds his own position turned, his plans frustrated and then reversed against himself before he realises precisely what game is afoot. He is swept off the board by a brilliantly executed version of Queen's Gambit Accepted.

In a previous chapter I drew attention to the Book of Judith. Judith, when the political and religious extinction of her people seemed both inevitable and imminent, walked openly into the enemy camp arrayed in her finest apparel. She was literally 'dressed to kill', for she had come to set what Le Carre would call a 'honey trap' for the Imperial Commander-in-chief, with herself as both bait and executioner. Hebrew literature, I think, endows its heroines with a degree of heroism beyond that of its heroes. I presume every Israelite male grew up knowing that he might one day be called upon to stand his ground, weapon in hand, 'facing fearful odds'. But nothing in the education of a Hebrew maid could have prepared an Esther or a Judith for the hair-raising situations in which they find themselves, which they face with intrepidity and in which they exhibit such a splendid sense of style.

To take another aspect of my theme; I watched with interest the other day a mimed version of the Fall, hastily improvised by some sixth formers. It confirmed what I have long thought: the man has a very thin part. The woman, in the centre of the stage listened with growing interest to the persuasions of the serpent and surveyed the tree with mounting appetite. She then munched an imaginary apple with a fine gusto, and passed one to the man, who only at this stage got into the act, and had nothing better to do than to try to bring equal relish to the eating of his own apple. Believe me, I am not trying to diminish the male responsibility for our fallen state. I am interested in the drama with which the writer invests the woman's choice, as I am interested in the name with which she emerges, 'Eve, because she was the mother of all living'.

That the woman is the channel of life is heavily and repeatedly emphasised in the patriarchal narratives. Abraham is told that Sarah 'shall be a mother of nations: kings of people shall come from her', a promise that both he and Sarah, in view of their age and childlessness find literally laughable. They are answered, 'Is anything too hard for the Lord?' Isaac is born, grows, marries and is also childless until, 'he prayed to the Lord . . . and the Lord granted his prayer, and Rebekah his wife conceived'. When their twin sons come of age, it is by the intervention of the mother Rebekah that Jacob, the younger, secures the senior's blessing and goes to seek a wife among their kindred. He marries Leah, whom he did not want, and Rachel whom he loves dearly. 'When the Lord saw that Leah was hated, he opened her womb; but Rachel was barren'. However, when Leah had born six sons, 'Then God remembered Rachel, and God harkened to her and opened her womb'. The text consistently speaks as though the life of this family is initiated, preserved and continued less by the seed of the Patriarchs than by the intervention of God in the lives of the womenfolk. The culmination comes in the New Testament, where a virgin asks, 'How shall this be, since I have no husband?' and receives the answer, '. . . the power of the Most High shall overshadow you . . . your kinswoman Elizabeth in her old age has also conceived . . . For with God nothing will be impossible'.

The gospel account of the Annunciation is surely meant to 'summon up remembrance' of the various women on whom the 'thin spun life' of Israel depended. As Mary listens to the angel's message that her son 'will be called holy, the Son of God', and expresses her acquiescence in whatever God should require of her, she stands in deliberate contrast to the erring Eve, who harkened to the serpents deceitful promise of divine status for herself and her husband, and forthwith flouted the divine prohibition. The angel's assurance that Mary's conception will be effected by the 'power of the Most High' is, as I have said, meant to evoke the memory of the Patriarch's wives. When the carpenter's betrothed is told that her son is 'to reign over the house of David for ever', I am put in mind of Esther and Judith, both abruptly called upon to save their entire nation from destruction. All three ladies rise to their high and terrifying destinies as three swans might breast unruffled the wavelets of a lake. And may I not include that Nausicaa of the Old Testament, who, beside the waters of the Nile, ensured that Israel's first deliverer and lawgiver should live?

# 'Gabriel, Make This Man Understand.'

*(Dan. 8.15.)*

In the haze of a late September evening an Oxford policeman observed a woman cyclist sedately riding a lampless machine along the centre of the pavement. 'I thought,' said the lady in answer to his expostulations, 'that I was safer riding on the pavement without lights than in the middle of the road.' Rather than discuss the presuppositions of that particular plea with a possible philosophy don, the policeman raised the simpler issue of lighting-up-time. 'I didn't expect to be out this late,' was the reply, 'but I went to Mass, and the priest preached for twenty-five minutes on the subject of the angels.' 'Well,' said the officer, standing back and allowing her to proceed. 'you certainly didn't make that up!'

Nor had she. I had been asked by the Catholic Graduate Society to say Mass and preach for them on September 29th, which, of course, is the feast of the three archangels. What, I had wondered, did these highly intelligent young Catholics think about the angels, supposing that they ever did think about them? Did they consider them to be a pious equivalent of the fairies? Did they find them intellectually embarrassing? Here was a challenge it would be ignoble to ignore. It proved a laborious one to have accepted. There are well over two hundred references to angels scattered over the entire Bible, and that is to omit cherubs, seraphs and principalities etc., whom we assign to the same order. The Fathers of the Church have a good deal to say about the angels; the mediaeval and later scholastic theologians assign them a key role in their systems, while Christian art has represented them differently at different times. So in the end that twenty-five minutes sermon was a feat of selectivity and compression.

At the moment I am conscious of a similar challenge, but fortunately of more limited scope. Last month I wrote of the Annunciation, and spoke exuberantly of the Old Testament heroines whom I see as symbolically present at that scene. I scarcely adverted to one of the two persons actually present, the one who speaks most of the lines, the angel Gabriel.

Gabriel first appears in the Book of Daniel. The prophet has just experienced a bewildering dream of a world-dominating ram challenged and destroyed by an even more powerful he-goat. 'When I, Daniel, had seen the vision, I sought to understand it; and behold there stood before me one having the appearance of a man. And I heard a man's voice... and it called, "Gabriel, make this man understand the vision."' The name Gabriel is variously translated. Some scholars say, 'hero of God'; others 'man of God'. However, since the word 'man' here resembles our use of it in 'play the man' or even 'you'll be a Man, my son', the difference is not great. I have also seen the translation, 'God is my hero'. Despite their differences all three interpretations are specifically masculine with a ring of soldierly fealty.

What of Gabriel's appearance? Daniel says, 'having the appearance of a man'. Once again the Hebrew word is firmly masculine. Of his second apparition he narrates: 'while I was speaking in prayer, the man Gabriel . . . came to me in swift flight.' 'Swift flight' suggests that he was winged, which is the way we normally depict an angel. Yet I can think of no other occasion in the Bible where an angel, as distinct from a cherub or seraph, is described as having wings. Moreover, some commentators say that 'in swift flight' is a misreading for 'in great weariness', and that these words apply to Daniel. In Chapter 10 an angel performing the same functions speaks to Daniel in exactly the same tones as Gabriel. The angel's appearance is described; 'a man clothed in linen, whose loins were girded with gold of Uphaz. His body was like beryl, his face like the appearance of lightning, his eyes like flaming torches, his arms and legs like the gleam of burnished bronze.' Do not try to imagine a pair of torches on a background of lightning! Rather, isolate each feature and assess the quality of the substance with which it is compared. Each is meant to be mightily impressive.

An angel is an impressive sight, inspiring awe and even terror. Daniel testifies that at the sight of Gabriel, 'I fell on my face in a deep sleep.' Samson's mother says of her visitant, 'his countenance was like the countenance of the angel of God, very terrible.' Cornelius, battle-hardened centurion, 'saw clearly in a vision an angel of God. And he stared at him in terror.' The angels carry with them something of the divine aura. No wonder. They belong to the divine entourage; they may be privy to the divine counsels; they are sometimes called 'the sons of God'. Luke's shepherds did not encounter a gaggle of insipid blond(e?) presences out carol singing. They beheld the ranks of a godlike aristocracy assembled on parade to honour a cotless baby. Diminish the angels and you weaken Luke's point.

Angels speak civilly to human beings; they instruct them; they assist them. They conduct themselves very much 'de haut en bas'. Gabriel speaks reassuringly to Daniel, picks him up off the floor and instructs him patiently. There is no doubt who is the superior being. He speaks to Zechariah from something approaching his full height, 'I am Gabriel, who stands in the presence of God.' And poor Zechariah is rendered speechless for the best part of a year.

How then should we visualise the Angel of the Annunciation, basing ourselves only on Scripture? Certainly not as one of those ladylike young men or bosomless winged pretties to whom pictures have accustomed us, but as unequivocally masculine with a suggestion of the elite warrior caste. Wingless, I think, for he is not a cherub. But make him as resplendent as you can. At the sight of this being, Daniel, who dared the lions and spoke the truth to kings, simply swooned. As with the angels of the Nativity, so with the Angel of the Annunciation. Angelic grandeur, seen first in contrast to the simplicity of the child or woman, and then as subordinate, is deftly deployed by the narrator to show the scale of the human being. So Gabriel, instructor of Daniel, silencer of Zechariah, presents himself to the North Country maid and addresses her with a deference no patriarch, prophet or priest ever knew from a divine envoy, 'Hail, O favoured one, the Lord is with you.' 'But she was greatly troubled at the saying and considered in her mind what sort of greeting this might be'. It is the message which bewilders her; the messenger she appears to take in her peasant stride. The scene is hers.

Lastly, Gabriel told Daniel that he had been sent to bring him 'wisdom and understanding'. He brought Mary and Zechariah a knowledge of their own role in God's salvific plan. 'Gabriel, make this man understand' is, of course, an imperative. Changing its tone to that of petition, I find it a worthwhile personal prayer.

# The Word and the Voice (1)

On Easter Sunday I went to the kitchen to enquire about John the Baptist. I did so, not in obedience to some curious local Eastertide observance, but because the Holy Week services being over, I now had a little time to devote to my next article, and the suzeraine of our kitchen is one of my principal hagiological consultants. Stepping with due deference into that world of briskly clattering heels, of overalls white enough to have served on Tabor and fearsome equipment docile in deft hands, I sought audience. 'Please, have you time to tell me what you think about John the Baptist?' Without a trace of decelerando in her work of creaming our Easter pudding, the lady delivered thoughtful judgement. 'Of course, he was overshadowed. He made things much easier for Our Lord. And I don't think that he is sufficiently venerated.'

Overshadowed? Perhaps I should adapt the metaphor to New Testament usage and say that he was outshone. Christ himself said of John, 'He was a burning and shining lamp.' Yet the same evangelist who reports that tribute, has already been at pains in the first verses of his gospel to state categorically, 'He was not the light.' For the Christian, John's lamp, brightly as it shone, is inevitably dimmed by 'the light of the world . . . the light of life.' Not that the gospel writers wish to belittle the Baptist. To reduce John's stature would be to diminish the force of his witness to Christ. At the same time their focus being on Christ, and their narrative skill considerable, they carry our minds, our imaginations and, where they succeed, our hearts to Christ. We may then come to think of John as a mere signpost, to be scanned attentively by those on the road, of no real interest to those who have arrived.

In the Fourth Gospel the Baptist reduces himself to something far less substantial than a signpost, to a mere sound echoing in the desert places. 'I am the voice of one crying in the wilderness.' Yet few voices in the ancient world attracted as many listeners, influenced as many disparate and unlikely people, formed as many minds or echoed as long in so many distant places. To listen to John among the rocks and stunted scrub came 'Jerusalem and all Judaea and all the region about the Jordan.' Matthew's list, enthusiastically though it reads, is incomplete. Galileans were to be found not only among the baptizands, but among John's disciples. Many 'who hungered and thirsted for righteousness' made the journey down into the Jordan valley, 1,000 feet beneath sea level with, if they were from Jerusalem, the long haul back over the Judaean highlands. So, more surprisingly, did the tax collectors, the soldiers and the lady friends of both. The men from the toll booths and the barracks asked how they might continue their professions and yet face with equanimity 'the wrath to come'. The courtesans, poor things, were faced with a starker choice. 'The tax collectors and the harlots believed him', Christ accused the Temple authorities, 'you did not.' In fact, according to Matthew, there were Pharisees and Sadducees who made the pilgrimage to the Jordan and even presented themselves to John for baptism, walking into a volley of vituperation very different from the compassionate moderation with which he counselled the revenue officials and the military.

So firmly did the Baptist establish himself in the esteem of the masses that Christ was able to floor the Temple authorities with the question, 'The baptism of John, whence was it?' They could not say it was of God; they dare not say that it was not. 'We are afraid of the multitude for all hold that John was a prophet.' At the opposite end of the social spectrum Herod the Tetrarch, shallow and self-indulgent, felt the force of this fearless ascetic. Constrained by the frankness of John's criticism to put him in prison, Herod nevertheless listened to him with respect, brooded bewilderedly on his sayings, and for a time 'kept him safe.' When Jesus of Nazareth's preaching and miracles give rise to wonderment and speculation some of the prophets jump to the conclusion that 'John the Baptiser has been raised from the dead.' Herod in his palace grasps at exactly the same explanation, 'John, whom I beheaded, has been raised.'

After John had been sacrificed to Herodias' malice and Herod's moral cowardice, his disciples 'came and took his body, and laid it in a tomb', a filial service which the crucified Christ was not to receive from the demoralised Twelve. These 'disciples of John', a coherent group, committed, austere, devout, offer impressive collective witness to the quality of John's formation. They fast; they pray. 'Lord' says one of the Twelve, perhaps a little enviously, 'teach us to pray as John taught his disciples.' Even after their master's ignominious end they do not falter in their allegiance, but continue to cherish his name and to spread the knowledge of his teaching and practices. Almost two decades later and several hundred miles away from the Jordan, in Pisidian Antioch, Paul of Tarsus addressing the local Jews will judge it politic to invoke the witness of John to Jesus. At a still later date, in the even more distant city of Ephesus, he will discover a congregation, to all appearances Christian, which has been baptised 'into John's baptism.' If he had travelled in North Africa or Mesopotamia would he have found the Baptist to be remembered, honoured and imitated any less than in Asia Minor?

My last witness, one not to be gainsaid, is Christ himself. He not only described John as a 'shining lamp', but also delcared him, 'A prophet, yes, . . . and more than a prophet.' In the vocabulary of Israel there could be no greater tribute. It puts the Baptist among, and even above, Samuel and Nathan, Elijah and Elisha, Isaiah and Ezechiel. At this period the term 'prophet' is used also of Abraham and Moses, because they converse with God. The prophet received 'the word of God' the most sacred of charges, and, in his own idiom, in terms of the contingent realities of his own times, conveyed it to Israel. The 'voice in the wilderness' did so with unprecedented power. Among the rich pastures of the New Testament it echoes still . . . 'He that hath ears to hear . . .'

# The Word and the Voice (II)

*He went away across the Jordan to the place where John at first baptised, and there he remained. And many came to him there (John 10.40).*

The sparsely populated scrubland where the followers of Jesus now found themselves, was very familiar to at least one of them. Andrew of Bethsaida actually belonged to the fertile valleys and wooded hills north of the Sea of Galilee. He had been drawn into this stony wilderness years ago by the Baptist's magnetic reputation, and once in that compelling presence, had elected to stay there, listening, dreaming, expectant. He might still have been there at the time of John's arrest, had not John himself realigned his life by directing his attention to a fellow Galilean, Jesus of Nazareth. I like to imagine Andrew recalling the occasion when he had done so.

Thank goodness John had indicated Jesus so explicitly. Without that prompting one would never have singled him out among the general melee of the curious, the penitent, the hero worshippers. John no-one could miss, with his primitive garments, if you could call them garments, hanging from that figure as gaunt as a ship's mast from a diet so primitive as to be practically prehistoric. He was plainly the focus of the coming and going, a second Elijah presaging Malachi's 'great and terrible day of the Lord.' There was nothing odd about Jesus's dress, nothing in the least way out about the food you had shared with him, when the pair of you had followed him and sheepishly accepted his invitation to his lodging, no atmosphere of 'the great and terrible' at all. Yet, when you had been some time in his company, you began to see him differently, to grasp something of what John had been talking about, and at the end of the session you found yourself with a new Master.

A new Master and an abrupt change in your way of life. With John you stayed by the Jordan. With Jesus you were for ever on tour. You marched back to dear old Galilee and then tramped its length and breadth, town by town, hamlet by hamlet, toured the lakeside settlements, and crossed and recrossed the Lake until even Tollhouse Matthew could tell port from starboard without working it out on his abacus. It was up to Jerusalem for the great feasts, and back again, with even the odd sally into largely gentile territory. John had stayed in this one area and let people gather to him. Jesus went where the people were already congregated, addressing them in the sabbath-filled synagogues and as they swarmed into the Temple at the height of the pilgrim season. He accepted every invitation into folk's houses, not just from friends, but from 'sinners', people normally shunned by the religiously observant, and even from Pharisees, at whose tables he reserved the right, if provoked, to speak his mind devastatingly.

Then there were miracles. Heaven knows it had been impressive enough to be with John and watch his effect on people, to see those revenue sharks and the thick-necked men-at-arms like hungry kids round the cooking pot, but begging for moral guidance, of all things, and quite sincerely too! It was something else altogether to be present when six great water pots, which you had just seen the servants filling from the well, turned out to be brimful of top quality wine; to watch several thousand people eat their fill from what had started out as one lad's rations; to see a bad case of paralysis turn as spry as a teenager, or a wild demoniac become every bit as quiet, as rational as yourself.

Living with John: following Jesus, those were two different worlds. Yet it was amazing to reflect how much John had achieved without seeming to try very hard. He had sought out nobody, made no use of synagogue or Temple, and still had large audiences out here in the wild. His appearance and his setting were hardly calculated to make anybody feel at home, but a surprising mixture of people took his words to heart, and he was never short of disciples. Even Herod — 'that fox', the Master called him, and Andrew had heard stronger expressions — was said to have listened to him in fascination. He worked no miracles, and yet was firmly established in the minds of the people as a prophet, as an authentic spokesman of the Lord God. Many had even surmised that he might be the Messiah.

What use had John made of all that influence, all that prestige? For himself, none at all. He had certainly cared for the people who came to him. To some he had delivered a blistering warning, 'Who warned you to flee from the wrath to come?' To the taxmen and the soldiers he had offered a code, one not observed by the majority of their colleagues, but still perfectly practicable, of no extortion and no false accusations. To the more idealistic he had urged, 'He who has two coats, let him share with him who has none.' If someone was willing to commit himself even further, he would teach him the discipline of prayer and fasting. He had seen himself as a messenger, one whose importance evaporates once the message is delivered and the recipient put in contact with the sender. He had called for a road to be built so that Israel and their God might come together. He was prepared to advise them how to make that road smooth and straight, and after that it was not for him to stand between those whom the road was intended to bring together.

The acclaim that came to him he had consistently directed elsewhere. 'After me there comes a man who ranks before me . . . the thong of whose sandal I am not worthy to untie.' He had trained disciples and then facilitated their transfer to Jesus. When those who remained with him complained of Jesus' mounting success he summed up the situation in the stark phrase, 'He must increase, but I must decrease.' Stark also had been the manner of that decrease, first mewed up in Machaerus like a criminal, and then executed because a woman hated him and a girl had danced prettily in front of Herod. The Baptist had, as it were, built up a foundation of religious expectancy, of sharpened moral awareness, of heightened spiritual idealism and then vacated the site for another architect to build thereon the New Jerusalem. He had not asked, and he had certainly not been granted, so much as a dignified exit.

The Baptist had taught Andrew to know his Saviour and to respond to him. He had also taught him, at least by example, to prepare people for the coming of Christ into their lives and then to quit the scene without making any claims on either party. Did Andrew draw that lesson? Quite a number of would-be-spiritual guides seem not to have done so.

# Herod the Half-hearted

*Herod feared John, knowing that he was a righteous and
holy man, and kept him safe. When he heard him he was
much perplexed, and yet he heard him gladly. (Mark 6.20)*

How very different from his father, Herod the Great, this
Herod Antipas is. Machaerus, the fortress-cum-palace in
which our scene is laid, had been built by the father. Massive in
its proportions, formidably fortified, excellently equipped
both as arsenal and royal villa, it was an uncompromising
assertion in stone of a king's power, of a realm's ample
resources, and Herod's determination to retain both. Half
Idumean, half Arab, with never a drop of genuine Israelite
blood in his veins, Herod had fought, intrigued and murdered
his way singlemindedly to the throne of all Israel. He had been
equally ruthless about staying there. He used spies, torturers
and the executioner to ensure his doing so. Even a wife — the
favourite, no less — three sons and a whole clutch of in-laws
had been pitilessly put to death. With those who were not
family, the male children of Bethlehem for example, his
methods were more wholesale.

Herod Antipas, by contrast, held his tetrarchy, a mere por-
tion of his father's territories, in virtue of his father's will and
the Emperor's ratification of it. To the Romans he had proved
satisfactorily subservient, to his neighbours for the most part
unprovocative, to his subjects, as rulers went, quite tolerable.
Twice in a reign of something like forty years he stirred up
trouble for himself. He did so when on a journey to Rome he
met Herodias, wife to his half-brother, Herod Philip. Forthwith Herodias abandoned Philip and Antipas his Nabatean
wife, thereby scandalising his Jewish subjects and making an

implacable enemy of his former father-in-law, the doughty King Aretas. Worse was to happen some years after the death of the Baptist. Agrippa, Herodias' brother, will receive the title of King. Herodias, keenly envious, will urge Herod to Rome to seek the same honour. There, quite out of his depth in a contest of intrigue with Agrippa, Antipas will not only lose, but find himself paying the unexpected forfeit of deposition and exile.

Herodias plainly, perhaps quite dazzlingly, is a key figure in both sets of events. She has not merely married into these Herodians, she is one of them by birth, a grandchild of Herod the Great, her grandmother being the murdered wife, Mariamme, her father one of the executed sons. From Mariamme may have come her power to fascinate Herod's son, from the founder of the dynasty that relentlessness of purpose so clearly lacking in Antipas. If an earlier Baptist had denounced King Herod, he would probably have been drowned in the river in which he baptised, and his disciples with him. Herodias is of the same cast of mind, but lacks the means to give it effect. Antipas, naturally, compromises. John is not executed, but imprisoned in Machaerus. He is not left to rot in some dungeon, but is brought from time to time to speak with the Tetrarch, who listens willingly, deferentially and, of course, inconclusively. One can feel almost sorry for this man trapped between the outspoken integrity of John and the malign pertinacity of Herodias. It was certainly an unkind fate which chose the night of his birthday party to impale him finally on the horns of his dilemma.

John the Baptist, as everyone knows, was danced to death by Salome, daughter of Herodias. There is no need to think of Salome as the statuesque witch of Beardsley's drawings. She was little more than a child. The dance, performed by a daughter of the ruling house at a public banquet, is unlikely to have been anything but decorous. Nor can I see any reason for crediting Herodias with a carefully laid, artfully sprung trap. More probably the daughter dashed into the room glowing from the plaudits of the guests, tense with excitement at the thought that she could have anything she asked for. He would have to give it. He had said it twice. He had sworn an oath. What should she say? Listening to this effusion, Herodias glimpses her prey out in the open and pounces. 'The head of John the Baptist, on a plate, now'. 'Now' because Herod must be allowed no chance to procrastinate. He must be made to choose on the spot with his guests, who are finding the after-dinner entertainment more interesting than they had anticipated, looking on eagerly. The Baptist must lose his life, or Herod lose face.

So John died to save Herod's face. It is true that he died because of the moral convictions which he felt obliged to voice, and because he had antagonised Herodias. However the order for his death was given so that Herod would not have to retract a drunken, extravagant promise. Similarly, we can say that Christ died to do his Father's will, or that he died for our sins, but the order for his death was given because Pilate chose to yield to the clamour of the Jewish leaders and their claque. Christ died to get Pilate out of a sticky situation.

Both decisions were taken by the man in the middle, a man who responded, however imperfectly, to the good, and yet betrayed it for rather contemptible reasons. There are other such 'men in the middle' in the Scriptures. Ahab, King of Israel, had a real, if grudging, respect for the prophet Elijah. Unfortunatey for many of Elijah's co-religionists Ahab allowed the heathen Jezebel to harry them mercilessly, while he looked to his chariot force. When Paul was in prison in Caesarea, the Governor, Felix, 'sent for him often and conversed with him', but 'desiring to do the Jews a favour, Felix left Paul in prison'. I wonder to myself whether in society at large the role of the 'man in the middle' is not often played by the general public, which has the last word but so often out of inertia, or conformism or sheer reluctance 'to become involved' signs with its silence the death warrant of the good. And how often is that middle man, not unattracted by the good, but rendered contemptible by his final choice, myself?

# 'Of Night and Light'

*Nicodemus also, who had first come to him by night, came bringing a mixture of myrrh and aloes, about a hundred pound in weight'. (John 19.39)*

This morning I went to the kitchen, where I asked to see a pound of spice. I was taken by the sovereign lady of that demesne to the furthest part of the larder and handed a half-pound of black pepper. After some discussion, I went to the sacristy, borrowed a packet of incense and then weighed it on the scales of our general office. The reason for these uncharacteristic forays into the empirical was that I wanted to be able to visualise seventy five pounds of myrrh and aloes. Only seventy five, because my Greek Lexicon informs me that the 'litra' of the text weighed only twelve ounces or 327.45 grams. I was trying to imagine the weight and bulk of that mixture of myrrh and aloes which Nicodemus brought to the burial of Jesus. I came to the conclusion that I myself would find such a load quite unmanageable, and permitted myself to wonder whether a man rich enough to provide so large a quantity of an expensive commodity, might not have had servants to carry it for him. This suggestion was firmly ruled out by the catering manageress, whose grasp of the essential proprieties is much surer than my own, on the grounds that a tribute of that sort on such an occasion could only be fittingly borne by the donor himself.

Was Nicodemus a powerfully built man? That, of course, is the kind of information which the gospel writers never give. They say not a word about the build and appearance of Christ, Mary or any of the Twelve. It is their words, their deeds, and only the most relevant, the most significant of those, which the evangelists are concerned to relate. In the eyes of John the significant detail about Nicodemus, it seems, is that 'he had at first come to him by night'. It is a dramatic detail. The tentative, clandestine nature of the eminent Pharisee's approach to the untrained, but startlingly impressive young preacher from the North, is caught in a single Greek word, 'nuktos'. Yet, as this is the Gospel of John, we are justified in looking for a deeper meaning.

In fact, we should look as far back as the second verse of Genesis. 'The earth was without form and void, and darkness was upon the face of the deep . . . and God said, "Let there be light" '. The first act of God is to create light, and thereafter nothing is more closely associated with Him than light, especially when He acts to save. It is from a flaming bush that He sends Moses to the oppressed Israelites, and as a pillar of fire that He subsequently leads them through the night to freedom. This association of illumination and salvation is celebrated by a later generation of Hebrews in the chant, 'The Lord is my light and my salvation'. In Acts, Peter lies in prison, doubly chained, quadruply guarded, when 'a light shone in the cell' and Peter is soon making his way freely through the streets of Jerusalem, chains, guards and prison gates left behind. In the New Jerusalem the saved 'need no lamp or sun, for the Lord God will be their light'.

John uses this association constantly in his presentation of the Saviour. The prologue declares, 'In him was life, and the life was the light of men'. At the Feast of Tabernacles Christ is shown in the Temple proclaiming, 'I am the light of the world'. Perhaps he made this assertion standing among the four great golden candlesticks which burned for the feast, just as in the first chapter of Revelation he appears amid the seven golden lampstands. Because in St. John the association of light and salvation crystallises into light and Christ, I suggest the word 'night' implies the absence of Christ. Thus, 'night comes when no man can work' refers both to death in general and to the limited duration of Christ's time on earth. When Judas turned his back on Christ at the last supper and went to perform his black treachery 'it was night'. In the final chapter Simon Peter and the others fish all the night without a catch, but at daybreak, enlightened by the Risen Lord, they immediately net more fish than they can take aboard.

Nicodemus I like to imagine standing at the threshold of the lamplit room, tense and solitary, hesitant yet urgent, behind him the dark backcloth of the night. His background is indeed dark. He is 'a ruler of the Jews', taking his seat in the Council alongside the highest ranks of the priesthood, the most influential rabbis, and the heads of the most powerful families. The 'true light' is shining upon Israel, and these, the men who should have been the best qualified to recognise it and to reflect it, are proving the most resistant, the least penetrable section of the nation. So Nicodemus stands framed in darkness, gazing hopefully into the light.

The darkness intensifies. The light can no longer be ignored. It must therefore be brought under control. The Council orders the arrest of Jesus. Nicodemus, growing in boldness, pleads, not yet for Christ, but for the light of impartiality. 'Does our law judge a man without first giving him a hearing?' Nicodemus does not speak again in the gospel. He acts. 'The power of darkness' prevails. The light is brutally extinguished, betrayed by one disciple, denied by the other, generally deserted. Nicodemus, once secretive and hesitant, at this the darkest point, salutes the Light with an unequivocal and glaring gesture, a hundred pounds of aromatic substance.

# Salome's Abortive Coup

*Then the mother of the sons of Zebedee came up to him and . . . she asked him for something . . . She said to him, 'Command that these two sons of mine may sit, one at your right hand and one at your left in your kingdom' (Matt. 20.20-2).*

My title could mislead. To the more romantic reader it might suggest that Herodias' daughter, bored with dancing, her ambition whetted by Herod Antipas' offer of 'Half my kingdom', subsequently attempted, no doubt with the help of some infatuated young Captain of the Guard, to unseat her adoptive father and seize the whole tetrarchy into her enchantingly expressive young hands. In fact, Herodias' daughter dances anonymously into the pages of the gospel and, having received the most incongruous dancing trophy in the history of the art, trips out again, her name still ungiven. The only Salome explicitly mentioned in the gospels is the wife of Zebedee, the Galilean fisherman. Zebedee himself appears but once. He forms part of the lakeside background with his boat, the hired hands and the half-mended nets, as his two lads fall in with Jona's two sons to trail after the magnetic, but apparently untrained, young rabbi from Nazareth.

That quartet, Simon and Andrew, James and John, are present when Jesus cures Simon's mother-in-law of her 'high fever', and much later, towards the end of Christ's ministry when the four of them beg to be told just when his horrifying predictions about the coming destruction of the Temple will come true. Andrew's presence at this late stage of the narrative gives one quite a surprise. When the Master made his way into the house of Jairus, thrusting aside the noisy so-called mourners, 'he allowed no-one to follow except Peter, James and John, the brother of James'. When he strode up the 'high mountain', there to be startlingly transformed into a figure of dazzling splendour, flanked by Moses and Elijah, he 'took with him Peter and James and John his brother'. At Gethsemane Jesus will take the same group of former fishermen with him, having expressly directed the others to 'Sit here, while I go yonder and pray'. Andrew is undoubtedly one of the Twelve whom 'he appointed . . . to be with him, and to be sent out to preach and have authority to cast out demons', but on the more significant occasions he is left behind, while the three men with whom he had pulled at the oars and hauled at the nets, go forward at the Master's heels.

Brother Simon on the other hand is not only present at all the select events, he seems to be the odds-on favourite to become the Number One among the Twelve. It is Simon who puts the questions, who is bold enough to express their misgivings, who, most important of all, can articulate their belief in the Master. He had done so at Caesarea Philippi and the Master had solemnly invested him with a new name, 'Rock'. That could be very significant. Father Abraham was once Abram; the ancestor Jacob had his name changed to Israel. True, the Zebedeans had also been given a name 'Boanerges', the 'Thunder Boys' or the 'Lightning Lads', but that was more of a nickname, surely, and a very apt one for people whose notion of proclaiming the Kingdom included taking out a hostile Samaritan village with celestial napalm!

So Andrew might speculate, ignorant of the future. Our difficulty, knowing something of later events, is to reconstruct the situation during Christ's lifetime. In the early chapters of the Acts of the Apostles, John is alongside Peter when he heals the lame beggar in the Temple, and when he subsequently faces the Sanhedrim. They go together to Samaria to invoke the Holy Spirit upon the Samaritan converts. (Fire from heaven after all!) And where is James? Yet in the synoptic gospels John is mentioned without James only twice. Usually he is mentioned after James, is often specified by reference to James as 'John his brother' or 'John the brother of James'.

You must reconcile the very unobtrusive, contemplative, intuitive companion of Peter — to whose robust impetuosity he is a clear foil — with the Thunder Boy, almost inseparable from, usually overtopped by, Brother James.

It is a relief to see sailing into these uncertain waters, a craft of very definite outline, steering a straight course for her chosen landfall. Somewhere west of Jericho, the matriarch Salome, the two Thunderboys reduced on this occasion to the role of attendant acolytes, presents her suit, 'that these two sons of mine may sit, one at your right hand and one at your left in your kingdom'. (These verses closely resemble I Kings 1.1ff. where Bathsheba demands the coronation of Solomon.) 'When the ten heard of it, they were indignant'. One would like to have seen their faces. To think of the woman demanding that the Master commit himself to her designs! Was Simon, who had led the field so long, to be ignored? Perhaps she would offer him the reversion of Zebedee's boat as a consolation prize. Imagine her James as Grand-Vizier-In-Perpetuity with John as deputy!

The Master, by contrast, remains unruffled. Salome is not chidden. Nor are her sons reprimanded, even though they have learned nothing from a similar previous occasion. Then he had placed a child 'in the midst of them, and said, "Whoever humbles himself like this child, he is the greatest." ' Now, gathering the bickerers about him, he rehearses the same lesson in other terms. 'Whoever would be first among you must be your slave; even as the Son of Man came . . . to give his life.'

When on Golgotha the Son of Man does give his life, quite unexpected patterns evolve. Salome, who had sought positions of honour only for her menfolk, stands on Calvary, utterly loyal to the very last, while the Twelve are dispersed and demoralized. Two dawns later, before any of them, she will know that 'He is risen'. Peter, who under pressure had collapsed shamefully, emerges a secure, unquestioned leader, with John, apparently, his chief support. James, once the principal challenger for the leadership, is listed in the Acts among those present in the upper room, and is mentioned only once again, 'Herod killed James the brother of John with the sword.' Of the Twelve, James **Bar** Zebedee is the first to 'give his life' for, and in imitation of, the Master, the first to enter into the fulness of the Kingdom. Salome's petition has received its divinely mutated fulfilment. I should never have called it 'abortive'.

# 'Just as the Women Had Said'
## (Luke 24.4)

*And coming up at that very hour she gave thanks to God, and spoke of him to all who were looking for the redemption of Israel. (Luke 2.38)*

'Once again it was a woman, you see! Not Simeon, but Anna. She told the people about Our Lord.' My biblical commentator on this occasion was a retired nun from a missionary congregation, her years many, her legs uncertain, her eyesight dim and barely preserved by a series of operations. I have been appointed to lead her through the Spiritual Exercises, and spend most of the sessions spellbound and awestruck, drinking in her observations. She is pithy: 'That clown Adam!', and profound: 'In the name of God', I asked, 'how could you spend all that time in that boring place Nazareth, when you had so much work to do? . . . Then I understood. God doesn't want our work, He wants our hearts.' She draws the gospel scenes against a background of rural Kashmir, explaining the focal importance of the village well, and the revolting feeding habits of the scavenging pigs. 'You would have to be very hungry to want to eat what they eat.' She spoke scathingly of the arrogant, merciless attitude of the menfolk to any woman they judged to have strayed, 'I know how they would treat Mary when she was found with child. And that poor Samaritan woman! But it was the woman who told them all about Our Lord and led them to him.'

As I write, our retreat is moving towards the end of the Public Life. I should dearly like to have had my retreatant's comments on the women witnesses to the Resurrection, the subject already chosen for this month's Reflection. Reading the Acts, I have been struck by Peter's stipulation for Apostle No. 12A. 'One of the men who have accompanied us during all the time that the Lord Jesus went in and out among us . . . one of these men must become with us a witness to his resurrection.' This, then, is the primary task of the Twelve, to witness to Christ's resurrection. To whom, however, had the Risen Lord first appeared? According to John, he first appeared to Mary Magdalen, a statement which is repeated in the addition to Mark, while Matthew adds 'the other Mary', as accompanying her. Who was the first to know the Lord had risen? According to Luke several women went to the tomb, to be told by 'two men in dazzling apparel', "He is not here, but has risen". Matthew names two women, Mark three, while in John, Mary Magdalen has this scene also to herself. In spite of these variations the synoptic gospels are quite self-consistent in that each gives the same list of women as going to the tomb 'on the first day of the week' as he has given for those watching the Lord's burial after having been present at his death. These women, therefore, witnessed Christ's death, and his burial, and were the first to be informed of his resurrection.

In Matthew and Mark they appear for the first time on Golgotha, although both gospels add that 'they had followed Jesus from Galilee, ministering to him.' Luke alone makes mention of them during the Galilean ministry. 'He went on through cities and villages, preaching and bringing the good news of the Kingdom of God. And the twelve were with him, and also some women . . . Mary, called Magdalen . . . and Joanna . . . and Susanna and many others, who provided for them out of their means.' A strange reversal of roles, with the males no longer the providers, but less remarkable than the fact of the presence of women in the entourage of an itinerant rabbi. Professor Jeremias describes it as an 'unprecedented happening.' 'It is suitable' said Philo, describing the mores of his fellow Jews, 'for women to stay indoors and to live in retirement'. The section of the synagogue where the scribes taught was closed to women, an attitude crystallised in the dictum of Rabbi Eliezer (c. 90 A.D.) 'If a man gives his daughter a knowledge of the Law, it is as though he taught her lechery.'

The Twelve had been publicly and specifically selected to be Jesus' constant companions, to be trained by that continual intimacy, by systematic instruction and supervised experience for their future mission. Constant companions? Not on Calvary! When Jesus hangs from the cross Judas has taken money to help put him there, the 'Rock' that was Simon has crumbled into perjured disavowal, while the rest 'forsook him and fled.' That inner core, so carefully built up, had disintegrated. It is the outer group of devoted women which stands firm, which literally takes its stand on Golgotha and holds it, which is present at the entombment, whence the Twelve are ignobly absent, in violation of one of the basic human pieties. Had these women any less cause than the Twelve for shock, bewilderment and disorientation? Did they perhaps retain one fixed point, their love for Jesus, that love which after the mandatory immobility of the Sabbath — the most demoralising part of the whole experience? — sent them back to the tomb to minister to him for the last time, there to experience that 'vision of angels, who said that he was alive'? It is, of course, the final irony of this whole situation, that the witness of women was *a priori* without validity in Jewish law.

When the Lord has been 'taken up', the Apostolic College begins to discharge its responsibilities. The reintegration of this body, admittedly minus one, the recovery of its cohesion, direction and confidence, is forceful evidence of the revivifying power of the Resurrection. At the same time we do well to remember, as they undoubtedly did, that they are a group of repentant deserters presided over by a contrite apostate. I am not denigrating the historic episcopate. I am suggesting that as the life of the Church begins with its leaders bitterly aware of their individual and group defectibility, their successors of the episcopate/presbyterate should preserve that awareness with regard to themselves almost as sedulously as the Faith itself. And we should also listen with discriminating avidity to those of either sex whose Christian insights spring from no sacramental commission, but simply from the loving service they have given to Christ. In becoming my retreatant's pupil, I am, for once in my life, doing something right.

# A Command Performance

*And Agrippa said to Paul, 'in a short time you think to make me a Christian!' And Paul said, 'Whether short or long, I would to God that not only you but also all who hear me this day might become such as I — except for these chains.' (Acts. 26. 28,9.)*

Paul was by this time a considerable connoisseur of audiences. He had been dealing with them for twenty years in a hundred different cities scattered over a dozen different provinces of the Empire. He had addressed himself to Jews and gentiles, to slaves and prosperous citizens, to fanatical mobs and to those supercilious philosophers in Athens. He had spoken in innumerable houses, in synagogue after synagogue, in market places by the Aegean, on the celebrated Areopagus — and that by invitation, if you please! and more recently from the steps of the fortress Antonia. He had even managed a few words in the Sanhedrim, on which his youthful ambitions had once been so confidently focussed. Good folk in many places had drunk in his words like parched travellers stumbling on an unexpected oasis; others had simply scoffed. The Athenian dilettanti had been airily dismissive, while the bitter hostility of so many of his fellow Jews was like an incurable wound. Porcius Festus, the host at this rather grand affair, was the fourth Roman governor he had met face to face. Sergius Paulus in Crete had been flatteringly receptive; at Corinth, Gallio would not allow him to utter a single word. Felix, Festus' predecessor, used to listen to him often, and with obvious interest, while Festus remained disdainfully unimpressed.

There was, nevertheless, a special flavour to this occasion, brought to it by King Agrippa, ruler in some of those northern territories, and his sister, Bernice. They were the great-grandchildren of Herod the Great and the Hasmonean princess, Mariamme. Their father, King Herod Agrippa, had ruled over practically all Palestine, and had been the intimate friend of two Roman Emperors, so that his children had received a Roman upbringing and possessed the entree into the very highest circles. They 'came with great pomp, and they entered the audience hall with the military tribunes and the prominent men of the city'. Paul felt no particular gratification at having attracted so imposing an audience. Nor was he especially humiliated at having to appear before it in chains. He had followed the crucified Messiah too long to be much affected by such considerations. Here was one more opprtunity to expound 'the Way', and he would grasp it with both hands.

That both those hands were at present encumbered by these clumsy irons was certainly a practical embarrassment. They impeded one's gestures; they swung distractingly and they clanked ludicrously. He could try ignoring them, but the spectators would still be put off by them. He might try freezing into total immobility, but he could no more address an audience without a flow of gestures than talk with his mouth closed. The artistry of Paul's solution delights me. There is no ignoring the chains, so he deliberately focusses on them. The audience and he are equally well aware of the things, so he purposely exploits them to establish another line of rapport. I like to imagine that Paul thrust his arms out wide as he said, 'not only you but also all who hear me this day', that he held the gesture for 'might become such as I', then paused, ruefully contemplated his ironware, and with a wry smile at the audience concluded, 'except for these chains.' Did Paul know that Agrippa's father had also had to wear a chain when he was imprisoned by Tiberius, and had been compensated for the indignity by Caligula, who presented him with a chain of gold equal in weight to the iron? Was he subtly reminding Agrippa that any man might find himself wearing such felon's gear?

Paul's next formal address is delivered in very different circumstances (Acts 28.17 — 22). He has been transferred from provincial Caesarea to the august City itself, where he awaits the result of his appeal to the Emperor. He is speaking not in Festus' audience chamber, but in the confined space of his own lodgings, where he lives under the guard of a single soldier. The audience consists not of visiting royalty and government officials, but of the leaders of the Jewish community in Rome. One detail remains unchanged; he is still shackled. In Paul's eyes this is the more important occasion. The good opinion of these men is of far more importance to him than the possible patronage of a half-heathen Herodian kinglet. To win them he must overcome two obstacles. The first is that he has been accused by Jews from Asia Minor and, more importantly, Jerusalem itself, of 'teaching men everywhere against the people and the law and this place (the Temple)'. Secondly, there is once more his chain. It is a real handicap because it will be a constant reminder to his audience that his case may yet terminate in his condemnation by the highest imperial authority. This was an aspect of the situation which these Jews as the leaders of a small, foreign, often suspect, minority could not afford to ignore.

As at Caesarea, so again in Rome, Paul's solution is bold, almost flagrant and very astute. The awkward factor, which a lesser man would wish to play down, even suppress, he displays in the most conspicuous place possible. He makes it the subject of his ending. I can almost see him brandishing the shackles as he concludes, 'it is because of the hope of Israel that I am bound with this chain.' He has used one difficulty to solve the other, then reversed the process. Is he a disloyal Jew? Absolutely not! He is so loyal to a Jewish vision that he is in chains. Is he a criminal that he is in chains? No! He is in chains soley because of his religious convictions. The rhetoric is a good deal stronger than the logic, but it would have been a very detached listener who registered the fact, and few Jews listened to Paul with detachment.

'No-one', says a modern scripture scholar speaking of Paul, 'questions his position as the most creative thinker in the history of Christianity.' Am I then culpably trivial in taking this Colossus among theologians, this greatest of missionaries, and interesting myself, and attempting to interest the reader in a mere oratorical ploy? I would plead that 'le style, c'est l'homme meme' and that style penetrates into the details of a man's performance. Would you encounter Paul's creativity? Would you appreciate his sense of the individual audience, and the immediacy of his response to it? Would you savour the elan with which he tackles every obstacle to the preaching of the Gospel? Then I will show you Paul in a handful of words. I think I have done so.

# The Signs of the Times

### —OR 'HERE BE DRAGONS'

To be strictly accurate, there is only one dragon: 'behold a great red dragon, with seven heads and ten horns, and seven diadems upon his heads. His tail swept down a third of the stars of heaven' (Apoc 12, 3-4). With destructive power of that order, one dragon seems quite enough, yet he summons to his aid a 'beast':

> And I saw a beast rising out of the sea with ten horns and seven heads, with ten diadems upon its horns and a blasphemous name upon its heads. And the beast that I saw was like a leopard, its feet were like a bear's and its mouth was like a lion's mouth (13, 1.2).

If you have a lively visual imagination you can easily overstrain it trying to bring all the bizarre equipment of these malefic beings into a passably harmonious composition. You are not meant to. The *London Punch* (an illustrated humorous magazine and an institution in Britain) once published a large coloured illustration of an old-fashioned poet down on one knee declaiming his verse enthusiastically to a handsome young woman. On her features was depicted no answering enthusiasm, but an expression of doubt verging on dissatisfaction and irritation. Above her head was a 'thinks' balloon, containing what one supposed was a raven's wing, two large stars beneath that, a tender rosebud beneath them and the whole formation somehow balanced upon a particularly undulant swan's neck. As we read the description of the beast, we must not commit the same solecism as the literal-minded young lady, and try to picture something looking like a leopard with the feet of a bear and the jaws of a lion. The description is not meant to tell us what the thing looked like; it is meant to give us some feel for its nature and disposition.

There are two things which the writers of the New Testament seem rarely to go for, physical descriptions and humour. Nowadays we want to be able to imagine people and things, and a modern press interviewer will always be careful to help us to do so: '...he received me in his small, brightly-painted fisherman's cottage, which looks across the grey waters of the estuary, his sixty years belied by his abundant and still dark hair, the eager, boyish sparkle in his clear green eyes and the lithe frame clad in a vivid red pullover and dark corduroy slacks...'. But you can comb the gospels and you will remain wholly in the dark as to whether Christ was tall or short, whether he was broad or slight of frame. You will not learn there what Mary looked like, or any of the Twelve. The Acts of the Apostles is equally devoid of material about the appearance of its chief characters or of the cities in which Paul preached and the lands through which he journeyed. This is not, I am sure, because the writers were interested only in the supra-mundane, or because their minds moved all the time on a higher plane. The Jews were a down-to-earth, physical people. They cared about appearances. Wily Herod knew what he was doing when he gave them one of the show-pieces of the ancient world as the setting for their already splendid rituals.

I suppose one always underestimates the economy forced on the New Testament writers; paper was expensive, penmanship a skilled craft. People were sparing with both. Paul, that passionate propagandist, was often prodigal with paper and his scribe's time, as he was prodigal of words, energy and emotional involvement, but he still concentrated on his religious message. Similarly intent, and much less exuberant, the other authors were very conscious of the need to be selective. 'There are also many other things which Jesus did; were every one of them to be written, I suppose that the world itself could not contain the books that would be written' (Jn 21,25). In those circumstances, perhaps we ought to be grateful that they did not have recourse to telegraphese! They do tell some stories at length. Luke, for instance, devotes as many verses to the story of the encounter on the road to Emmaus as he spends on the story of the Passion from Pilate's verdict to Jesus's last breath. This he does because his readers knew what happened when a man was crucified, and there was no need to tell them, whereas most of them found it quite unimaginable that a man who had been crucified could be the Messiah and Saviour; so it is to this aspect of his message that Luke, like his colleagues a devoted pedagogue, addresses himself. When these men write they are teaching, preaching, explaining, persuading, warning. They are not compiling an interesting record; they are not trying to entertain. So we shall never know what any of the gospel characters looked like.

There is one description of Christ in the New Testament. He is seen in a vision by the same seer whom I have quoted about the dragon and the beast. 'His head and his hair were white as white wool, white as snow, his eyes were like a flame of fire, his feet were like burnished bronze, refined as in a furnace, and his voice was like the sound of many waters...' (Apoc 1, 14-15). That, of course, tells you nothing about Christ's appearance. It is a densely woven tissue of symbols, all borrowed from the Old Testament prophets and quite familiar to many of the seer's readers. It is an attempt to describe not an appearance, but a significance. It communicates Christ's grandeur and glory. It is particularly eloquent in that most of the symbols originally occur in Old Testament visions of the Deity. The technique here is to communicate non-visual qualities through easily-imaginable symbols such as snow, flame and bronze. Readers familiar with the Hebrew prophets would be quite at home in interpreting such symbols in terms of Christ's status and mission, and were presumably content to remain wholly uninformed about Christ's stature and lineaments.

To me, a greater deprivation than the lack of physical descriptions in the New Testament is the comparative rarity of humour. Humour is no trivial element in our lives. It is a prerogative of man, which the brute creation does not share. It springs from our intelligence, our imagination and creativity. It eases tension, defuses hostility, creates rapport between individuals, enriches friendship, makes the unpleasant a little more tolerable and renders the agreeable even more enjoyable. It also provides an effective test of the genuine. True dignity, real worth can tolerate being made fun of: portentousness and pretence never. Shakespeare can put broad farce into a play, and the impact of the drama and the power of the poetry suffer nothing from the juxtaposition. The writers of the New Testament do not mix their genres in this way.

Would that they did! Relevant again here is my previous remark that I must be grateful that they did not write in telegraphese. In the gospels and in the epistles there is great urgency. The writers are possessed by an imperative need to communicate their knowledge. They narrate, explain, argue and persuade, but, unlike Shakespeare, they are not writing to entertain; they are not concerned to produce literature. What they have to say has more in common with the matter of an urgent telegram than with the elements of deliberate literary creation. In their urgent concern to communicate, they frequently achieve vivid narrative, trenchant exposition and pithy and even pungent comment, but not humour.

I believe that I can see traces of Christ's humour here and there in the gospels. I think that I can detect it in some of the parables, in some of his verbal sparring, in the fact that he gave nicknames to the Sons of Zebedee. (Did he have nicknames for all the Twelve?) I don't know whether Luke meant us to smile when he tells us about the young man who fell asleep during Paul's all-night sermon, or about the maid who left Peter locked out: a story which is all the more pleasant when you remember that iron gates and four squads of four soldiers had not been able to keep Peter in prison, but the oversight of an excited girl could keep him cooling his heels on a domestic doorstep. I am reasonably confident that Paul, who seems to have been able to pull out every other oratorical stop, could amuse when he wanted. In the book 'Revelation', however, biased though I am in its favour, I can detect not a mote of humour, nor the slightest trace of any.

This total absence of humour is not the only unattractive aspect of this particular inspired book. Its symbols, although I think that I have trained myself to appreciate them in some degree, strike many a reader as naive (dragons, forsooth!), lurid and frustratingly obscure. Worst of all, the theme of the book seems so repetitiously vengeful. One groans, not with terror but with tedium, as the umpteenth angel sounds yet another trumpet, or empties out one more bowl of the vengeance of God upon the wicked, so that they are afflicted by still another hideous plague or struck by some new cosmic cataclysm, 'and blood flowed from the wine press (of the wrath of God), as high as a horse's bridle for one thousand six hundred stadia' (14,20). Imagine that!

I received some enlightenment in this matter more than fifteen years ago from half a dozen small children. I found myself watching part of a television version of *The Old Curiosity Shop*. In this episode the odious dwarf, Daniel Quilp, met his end. We watched him fleeing from his pursuers through the dense fog, unable to see more than a few inches in front of him. Totally lost, he topples into the river, where he frenziedly tries to keep himself afloat, unable to tell where the bank might be. His terror, his panic, was very effectively conveyed and I sat there horrified. Not so the children who, as Quilp went down for the last time, let out a unanimous and spontaneous cheer. I had been watching a horrible death. They had seen an evil man, who had been responsible for the sufferings of Little Nell and others, destroyed by his own machinations. The good were delivered from him, and, except for poor Nell, could now live happily ever after. This was worth a cheer.

The story of the triumph of good over evil has many literary forms, but the message remains the same. Good prevails; evil is defeated, and if in such stories evil is personified in the villains, the defeat of evil is spelled out in the villains' death. With our modern sensitivity we might prefer conversion stories, and I should have found it easier to watch Quilp won over to a life of honesty and philanthropy, but I don't think that the children would have been moved to cheer.

And if we were to rewrite all the epics as conversion stories, with Goliath becoming an ambassador of goodwill between the Philistines and the Hebrews, and the ranks of Tuscany deciding to give Rome's new experiment in republican government their economic and diplomatic support, would anybody re-tell the stories? I doubt if you can tamper with a literary form and preserve its vitality. And 'Revelation' is a piece of highly imaginative literature to be understood only within its own conventions.

I described 'Revelation' as tediously vengeful. Even if one can reconcile oneself to the mythological requirement that the forces of evil should be resoundingly defeated, it is still wearisome to have that defeat re-staged so often. Must there be another plague, another vast battle, more fire from heaven every time I turn a page? As a used-up schoolmaster I recognize the technique, even if I do not enjoy it, and I am constrained to acknowledge its necessity. You may convey a piece of factual knowledge by stating it once. If it is an essential piece of knowledge you must see that it is re-stated, perhaps in different forms, so often that it cannot be forgotten. If a truth is to be absorbed into the imagination, to be appreciated and felt, to become an important part of the hearer's outlook, it will usually have to be presented several times, and preferably in a variety of ways. This is what the author of 'Revelation' is trying to do. If I do not like his idiom and technique, then I must abstract the truth he is so concerned to teach, and go on to find my own way of impressing it on my imagination and digesting it into my general religious outlook, while remaining grateful to the book for stating that truth and conveying its urgency and importance. Nevertheless, to understand the author's technique is not necessarily to enjoy it, and his litany of cataclysms and hecatombs becomes no more palatable because I understand what it is doing there.

Yet 'Revelation' is the section of the Bible outside the gospels which I have most often read, which I have most studied—entirely voluntarily—and which has most influenced my thinking. Its symbols, since I came to some minimal understanding of them, intrigue me, and in that I am not alone. 'Revelation' is a favourite source for mosaics, stained glass and representation in almost every medium. I say 'almost' because I can remember no sculptural expression of any of its scenes, other than Epstein's splendid Michael at Coventry. As one becomes attuned to the book it turns out to be vivid, dramatic and beyond doubt the product of literary genius. The structure is fascinating: the deployment of *dramatis personae* and the unrolling of events superbly controlled. Detailed comment, as I am not writing a piece of literary criticism, I must waive, with only passing mention of its magnificent 'diptychs'; the 'Woman clothed with the sun, with the moon under her feet, and on her head a crown of twelve stars' (12,1), over against the 'great harlot', 'sitting on a scarlet beast, arrayed in purple and scarlet and bedecked with gold and jewels and pearls' (17,4); the dragon with his attendant beasts and their branded subjects, balanced by the triumphant Lamb and the multitude of the redeemed 'who had his name and his Father's name written on their foreheads'. And I must mention the extraordinary dramatic pauses which the author inserts into the almost headlong action. Thus, when events unroll in their sevens, there is commonly inserted between the sixth and the climactic seventh a double scene of quite different pace and character; and I am always fascinated by that riveting insertion, 'when the Lamb opened the seventh seal, there was silence in heaven for about half an hour' (8,1).

My relish for Revelation's literary qualities I admit to be an acquired taste, a by-product, as far as I am concerned, of the laborious effort to penetrate to the author's message. The book is providentially the last work in the Bible. Apparently it was by no means the last piece of the New Testament to be written, yet there it is, having, as it were, the last word, and I want to know what that last word contains for my enlightenment and guidance. Paradoxically, I think that it fits particularly well at the end of the New Testament because of its continual references to the Old. The roots of 'Revelation' reaching back through Daniel, Ezechiel and Exodus to Genesis itself—I am always pleased to see that reference to the 'tree of life' in Revelation's last chapter—seem to me to help to bind

the whole corpus of scripture together. I also enjoy the gleam-
ing, glittering metamorphosis of Jerusalem in the penultimate
chapter, which provides a glorious ending for the city con-
quered by David, embellished by Solomon, ravaged by
Babylon, rebuilt by Nehemiah; the city in which Christ died
and the Church was born.

Yet it is not for the pleasure of contemplating the New
Jerusalem that I re-read 'Revelation', nor out of partiality for
dragons, nor even to savour the apocalyptic choreography. I
read therein in the hopes of absorbing the final message of the
New Testament, and because I believe that final message to
have been delivered to people whose situation was fundamentally our own, whose needs therefore closely resemble our
needs, who in that situation and among those needs were given
guidance which we also ought to attend to and follow. 'Revelation' was addressed to people who for the most part were born
after Christ had died, who were living when those who had
known Christ were dead, who were practising Christians when
the first great Pentecostal wave had already passed, to people
who, adapting John's words, 'had not seen and yet believed'.
The book is written to people who have been Christians for
some time, members of congregations established not at all
recently, believers for whom the good news of the gospel was
not at all new.

Chapters two and three show us to what manner of Christian 'Revelation' was first addressed. These chapters, in strong
contrast with the rest of the work, are wholly free from spectacle and melodrama. Not a trumpet sounds, not a single flash
of lightning is to be seen, as each of seven local churches
receive their messages. The chapters are not flatly prosaic;
each message begins with some detail skilfully linking it to the
initial vision of Christ, and concludes with a different and
highly imaginative symbol of salvation, my favourite being
that held out to Thyatira, 'and I will give him the morning star'
(2,28). But the messages themselves are terse and telling,
whether for praise or censure. The Churches are judged as to
whether they have shown themselves faithful and persevering
in the face of hostile pressure. This is not a matter merely of

persecution from without, a serious enough matter in itself indeed, but of perverted teaching within the congregations and, most malignant of all, the fading of their own vision, and the attrition of their personal commitment to Christ.

It is for failings under this last heading that censure is at its most severe. 'Because you are lukewarm, and neither cold nor hot, I will spew you out of my mouth', the Laodiceans are told (3,15). Sardis, even more sternly, 'you have the name of being alive and you are dead' (3,1). Much-praised Ephesus is told with compassionate rigour, 'I have this against you, that you have abandoned the love you had at first' (2,4). As for false teaching among these churches, we have clear evidence of its existence and precious little about its nature. Ephesus is praised for its resistance to the 'Nicolaitans', Sardis is warned about their presence and also of that of people 'who hold the teaching of Balaam', while Thyatira is reprimanded because 'you tolerate the woman Jezebel, who calls herself a prophetess' (2,20). Similarly, it is clear that these Christians experience persecution, but it is not always clear who persecutes them and by what means. For two congregations the hostility of the local Jews is a serious factor, but we are not told what form it took. At Pergamum, 'Antipas, my faithful one, has been put to death' (2,13), but we are not told how, or by whom. Smyrna is warned, 'the devil is about to throw some of you into prison' (2,10), but we do not know who acted for the devil on this occasion, nor on what grounds. When the churches are commended, the virtue most frequently mentioned is 'patient endurance'. For this, Ephesus, Thyatira and Philadelphia are praised, and it is to the same virtue, phrased a little differently, that they are urged. 'Hold fast what you have', Smyrna, Thyatira and Philadelphia are exhorted; but to Smyrna are addressed the still graver words: 'Be faithful unto death' (2,10).

These early christian congregations were obviously small affairs, and their members people of little consequence even in their own environment. So weak was their position that even the Jews could seem formidable enemies, although themselves outsiders in those cities, regarded with suspicion and sometimes the victims of anti-Jewish riots. Most frightening could be the hostility of pagan fellow-citizens, while the possibility of an imperial persecution must have been horrifying. For the Christians, dragons and ten-horned beasts did stalk the world. Indeed, the combination of ten horns, a bear's paws and a lion's jaws hardly does justice to the fell power of Rome when wielded by a Nero or a Domitian. And we must keep it in mind that persecution was only one of the dangers which menaced them. What are they to do about Nicolaitans and other purveyors of unchristian doctrine? At that early period of the Church's evolution, both doctrinal and organizational, were the doctrines of the Church formulated explicitly, and definitively enough, and authority within the local church so clearly assigned, that it was quite clear who should pronounce in matters of orthodoxy and what steps they should take to preserve it? Or were the congregations often a prey to dissension and bewilderment, because authoritative formulation or doctrine and the structure of jurisdiction were still rudimentary?

How exposed those early Christians were! 'Revelation' has a terrible picture of exposure, of total vulnerability; the dragon, his tail having just swept a third of the stars of heaven out of the sky, 'stood before the woman who was about to bear a child, that he might devour her child when she brought it forth' (12,4). That verse chills my blood at every reading; to me it presents the defencelessness of Christ more piercingly than Isaiah or the Passion narratives. Actually, in 'Revelation' at this point there is no reference to the crucifixion, and the child is 'caught up to God and to his throne' (12,5). The woman, who apparently stands both for Israel and the Church, is the next target of the dragon's malice, and she also is preserved by special intervention. 'Then the dragon was angry with the woman, and went off to make war on the rest of her offspring, on those who keep the commandments of God and bear testimony to Jesus' (12,17). The Christians of Ephesus, Pergamum and the other cities must have been able to hear those dragon-feet padding all around them, and imagined that catastrophe-dealing tail curving over their heads.

126

I said above that the situation of those early Christians was 'fundamentally our own'. We live, as they lived, between the death of Christ and his second coming, and in that long age the dragon walks, and we also are children of the Woman. The fact that there are hundreds of millions of baptized members of the Church, and the people of the Seven Churches could have been accommodated in one of our cathedrals with room to spare, does not make us the less exposed. 'For you say, I am rich, I have prospered, and I need nothing; not knowing that you are wretched, pitiable, poor, blind and naked' (2,17). Few things are as debilitating as complacency. The dragon has not gone to sleep in our time because I am not likely to be mauled to death by lions in the arena. The dragon's tail has dealt roughly enough with the Church in China, and in most countries beyond the Iron Curtain her life is restricted and opposed, while the Caesars of the Kremlin and their client courts remain capable of ruthless repression of a sort to make the efforts of Julian and Flavian Emperors look amateurish and half-hearted.

Then there are large areas of the world where the mass of the population has been duly baptized into the Church, where heads of governments may attend the *Te Deum* ordered for the celebration of the anniversary of their seizure of power, where a prevailing Voltairean scepticism does not inhibit public politeness to clerics and religious; and it is only when they speak too pointedly about rights and justice that they are denounced as communists, perhaps imprisoned, possibly murdered. As I sit here this Easter Sunday scribbling these reflections, I am not likely in the immediate future to be arrested for priestcraft, or imprisoned for my occasional anti-capitalist mutterings; but I should be very naif if I thought that in our tolerant, pluralist climate the dragon cannot, or does not, prowl. I must teach myself to remember that in the messages to the Seven Churches the threat of persecution, which would seem to us easily the worse menace on their horizon, though clearly forecast, receives less emphasis than their internal weaknesses.

Catholics, although aware of their individual frailty, used to feel secure in the Church. In the course of centuries of controversy, the One True Church had evolved a network of systematic formulae to express true christian doctrine neatly, precisely and permanently. The formulae were there to be consulted admiringly in seminary textbooks, in digests of Catholic Doctrine and in the Catechism. Catholic moral teaching had been similarly codified, and confessors were trained not only to know and apply their 'moral' compendia, but also to recognize the more subtle and unusual issue and seek its solution from the specialist. There always was a solution, for we enjoyed an infallible guide in faith and morals. We knew where to look for authoritative teaching; we were equally clear about matters of discipline. The Pope ruled the Church and the bishops their dioceses under him. Canon law, the decrees of Roman Congregations and *ad clerum* letters told us what we might do and not do. Authority was plainly identifiable and our discipline outstanding, as behoved the Church Militant, with its members always on active service in a truceless war.

The security conferred by that kind of clarity, that brand of certitude, is now lost to us. Theologians point out to us that the same words do not say the same things to different generations, that words 'slip, slide, perish, decay with imprecision', that much of our theological terminology, many of our theological concepts, rest on a philosophical system we no longer hold. No verbal expression, they rightly point out, can capture and imprison for ever the essential truths concerning God and Man. Manfully the theologians labour to find new *points de depart*: to harness contemporary philosophies, to produce new terminologies where necessary, and to correct the over- or under-emphases of the past. Unfortunately all this is a very esoteric affair, and those of us who have to keep asking someone else to remind us which is existential and which is ex-isten*tiel* soon get quite lost. We also, as happens when people get lost, get frightened. Have these exploratory theologians been courageous or presumptuous? Are they carrying out re-adjustments or demolitions? Are the doctrines of the Divinity of Christ, Papal Infallibility, the Real Presence, the *ex opere operato* effect of the sacraments still held by them? To some of us heresy would seem to have taken over; I myself just wonder at times whether the attempt to re-interpret the Faith for Contemporary Man has done anything except re-interpret it to the re-interpreters.

Traditional moral theology — by which I do not mean traditional christian morality, but our attempt to systematize and codify it — has slipped and slid. It is to be hoped that it does not perish before we have found a new set of tools to do its work. Traditional sexual morality is being 're-interpreted' not so much by theorists, although these are at work, as by a good deal of very down-to-earth, grassroots activity. It is nothing new for people to break the rules; it seems to me new for them to repudiate the rules, as do some practising Catholics in the matter of re-marriage after divorce, and many young Catholics in the matter of pre-marital sex. The tangle over contraception exhibits our confusion over both moral theology and doctrinal authority. Ecclesiastical authority reiterates traditional teaching and is frequently disregarded, not simply out of wantonness, but because the location of authority has now become unclear. The centralized absolutism of the Vatican is no longer accepted unhesitatingly. Many want to see the regular, genuine, untrammelled exercise of the collective responsibility of the episcopate, and would like to see the views of theologians, the pastoral experience of priests and the moral discernment of conscientious and mature lay people counting for a very great deal more in the deliberations of the Church. Some unfortunate people, misunderstanding the phrase 'you must follow your conscience', have simply become their own popes. So what was an absolute monarchy has become somewhat diluted with oligarchy, distracted with demands for a generous measure of consultative democracy, and has degenerated at the fringes into sheer anarchy.

Catholics who greatly prized their former security (is St Linus their patron?) are sincerely scandalized. The exploratory theologians seem to them heretics and propagators of heresy, and the revisionists in moral theology to have surrendered to pagan standards, or the lack of them; authority has failed in its responsibility to govern, and the rest of us have been found wanting in the key virtue of obedience. The liberals or progressives are, I think, a shade less demoralized, but quite as discontented. Episcopal synods, diocesan commissions, parish councils seem to them placatory gestures rather than genuine instruments of consultation. So it is with many other reforms which they find partial and inconclusive, tantalizing rather than satisfying. Their picture is of the upper echelons of the celibate, clerical hierocrats tenaciously preserving all they can of their own power and of the outlook and practices which sustain it. The rest of us they blame not for disobedience, but for apathy and acquiescence. It would be nicely comforting if I could say that these two pictures are so opposed to one another that they neatly cancel each other out, showing that the Church has conducted herself with sensible moderation, surrendering to neither extreme and proceeding at a controlled pace acceptable to the bulk of her members. That would be to kid ourselves. I am not claiming that the pews are smouldering with resentment either at past glories wantonly demolished or at visions of the future now dimmed and deferred. There is an awareness of the deep inconsistency between the reaffirmed teaching of *Humanae Vitae* and the conviction and practice of most western Catholics. There is some unease, sometimes degenerating into cynicism, though I could not estimate its scale, about a resolute opposition to remarriage after divorce and a multiplication in our time of decrees of nullity. Many older members of the congregation have been saddened by the failure of priest, school and family to prevent the defection of their children from the Church. They are also painfully aware of their own and everybody else's inability to state traditional christian sexual morality in a way which their children find even half convincing.

One result of clerical celibacy, which I think does not receive sufficient attention, is that priests come from lay families — or not at all. Priestly recruitment thus becomes some sort of index of the degree of commitment in the pews. What depressing comment then comes from the present state of recruitment to the priesthood and to the religious congregations! I would not dare to say whether this indicates a lukewarmness of christian faith or simply a want of confidence in its traditional institutions. The first explanation would be more disquieting than the second; either is dismaying. I have sometimes consoled myself with the notion, which I am far from renouncing, that Providence is calling the Church to produce new forms of ministry, new forms of dedication. In that case I must also believe that in its rigid adherence to the seminary-trained celibate as the only acceptable presbyteral form in the western Church, and in its obstinate preservation of a male monopoly of the ministry even as far down as formal acceptance to lectorship, ecclesiastical authority is resisting Providence to the considerable impoverishment of the Church. And I do not find that a consoling deduction.

It is symptomatic of our time that we speak a great deal less of the Church Militant and would rather employ the phrase 'the Pilgrim Church'. The latter model is surely more consonant with gospel ideas and certainly expresses the decrease in our sense of security. Any dragon with sense would pass up a well-equipped, well-drilled fighting unit in favour of mauling a huddle of pilgrims. Is this decrease of confidence in our organization a real deterioration? Or is a high degree of exposure, reaching its apogee in the picture of the Woman about to give birth, the right situation for Christians, linking us not only with the Woman, but more importantly perhaps with the Lamb?

I have suggested that the Church in our day, with its millions of members, experiences something of that same vulnerability of which the Seven Churches, with the exception of the smug folk of Laodicea, must have been so apprehensively aware. They knew persecution, and so do large areas of the Church of the twentieth century. They had problems with regard to orthodoxy and organization; so, to a degree which the Ultramontane Church of my youth would never have expected, do we. Yet it was not the open persecution of the Christians which most concerned him 'who holds the seven stars in his right hand', nor was it the damage inflicted by 'those who call themselves apostles, but are not' (2,2), or by Jezebel or the Nicolaitans. The profoundest warnings deal with the robustness, or rather the lack of it, of what we might nowadays call the commitment of these early Christians. It is

the vigour of their faith or its weakness, the vitality or otherwise of their loving adherence, which is the key issue in
Christ's assessment of them. Judged by this criterion would we
be found to stand in less peril than the folk of the Seven
Churches? They lived as a tiny minority in a pagan world; we
of the modern West exist in a world which has been called
post-christian, which certainly seems to retain less of its christian past with every successive decade. Which situation is the
more debilitating to faith, hope and charity? The world of the
first Christians was pagan, but it was religious. Our world
withdraws from Christianity into irreligion. The first-century
Ephesian may have breathed an atmosphere of paganism, but
it did not come at him from his TV set and the weekly
periodical and with all the vivid immediacy of the so-called
'media'. The natural scientists had not presented him with a
world picture of an unimaginable vastness and complexity to
make religious thought seem a quaint collection of primitively
naive concepts. That Ephesian did not have to ask himself
whether psychology and sociology do not give much more in-
sight into how a man should live and how society should conduct itself than does the Bible. He had not had the experience
of seeing regularly observant Christians allowing their actions
and attitudes to be dictated, not by gospel principles but by
racial prejudice, irrational, nationalist emotion or economic
self-interest. I am not arguing that our situation is worse than
that of the Christians of the Seven Churches. I do maintain
that we are no less exposed to demoralization. First century or
twentieth, we all of us make good dragon's meat.

*Rules for Dealing with the dragon*

1. *Admit he is there.* Acknowledge, objectively but compas-
sionately, the weaknesses of the Church. Assess honestly and
penitently 'your works, your love and faith and service and patient endurance' (2,39), or the lack of them.

2. *Do not be surprised.* We are children of 'the Woman'; we
are followers of 'the Lamb who was slain'. What did you expect?

3. *Don't run away.* Here the laws of the Looking Glass World apply: Run away and you have walked into his jaws. 'Hold fast what you have!' (2,25)

4. *Remember that if you stand firm and he devours you, it is he that will die of it.* This is the law of the Resurrection. 'Be faithful unto *death* and I will give you the crown of *life*'. (2,10)

5. *Study 'Revelation'.* Absorb the very direct and simple advice given to the churches in the early section. Wrestle with the apparently complex symbolism (it is rather fun). Learn to be patient with its restatements of the same point. Most of all, digest its principal lesson: It is the dragon who is doomed.